C-3833   CAREER EXAMINATION SERIES

This is your
PASSBOOK for...

Bail Bond Agent

Test Preparation Study Guide
Questions & Answers

COPYRIGHT NOTICE

This book is SOLELY intended for, is sold ONLY to, and its use is RESTRICTED to individual, bona fide applicants or candidates who qualify by virtue of having seriously filed applications for appropriate license, certificate, professional and/or promotional advancement, higher school matriculation, scholarship, or other legitimate requirements of education and/or governmental authorities.

This book is NOT intended for use, class instruction, tutoring, training, duplication, copying, reprinting, excerption, or adaptation, etc., by:

1) Other publishers
2) Proprietors and/or Instructors of "Coaching" and/or Preparatory Courses
3) Personnel and/or Training Divisions of commercial, industrial, and governmental organizations
4) Schools, colleges, or universities and/or their departments and staffs, including teachers and other personnel
5) Testing Agencies or Bureaus
6) Study groups which seek by the purchase of a single volume to copy and/or duplicate and/or adapt this material for use by the group as a whole without having purchased individual volumes for each of the members of the group
7) Et al.

Such persons would be in violation of appropriate Federal and State statutes.

PROVISION OF LICENSING AGREEMENTS – Recognized educational, commercial, industrial, and governmental institutions and organizations, and others legitimately engaged in educational pursuits, including training, testing, and measurement activities, may address request for a licensing agreement to the copyright owners, who will determine whether, and under what conditions, including fees and charges, the materials in this book may be used them. In other words, a licensing facility exists for the legitimate use of the material in this book on other than an individual basis. However, it is asseverated and affirmed here that the material in this book CANNOT be used without the receipt of the express permission of such a licensing agreement from the Publishers. Inquiries re licensing should be addressed to the company, attention rights and permissions department.

All rights reserved, including the right of reproduction in whole or in part, in any form or by any means, electronic or mechanical, including photocopying, recording, or by any information storage and retrieval system, without permission in writing from the Publisher.

Copyright © 2024 by
National Learning Corporation

212 Michael Drive, Syosset, NY 11791
(516) 921-8888 • www.passbooks.com
E-mail: info@passbooks.com

PASSBOOK® SERIES

THE *PASSBOOK® SERIES* has been created to prepare applicants and candidates for the ultimate academic battlefield – the examination room.

At some time in our lives, each and every one of us may be required to take an examination – for validation, matriculation, admission, qualification, registration, certification, or licensure.

Based on the assumption that every applicant or candidate has met the basic formal educational standards, has taken the required number of courses, and read the necessary texts, the *PASSBOOK® SERIES* furnishes the one special preparation which may assure passing with confidence, instead of failing with insecurity. Examination questions – together with answers – are furnished as the basic vehicle for study so that the mysteries of the examination and its compounding difficulties may be eliminated or diminished by a sure method.

This book is meant to help you pass your examination provided that you qualify and are serious in your objective.

The entire field is reviewed through the huge store of content information which is succinctly presented through a provocative and challenging approach – the question-and-answer method.

A climate of success is established by furnishing the correct answers at the end of each test.

You soon learn to recognize types of questions, forms of questions, and patterns of questioning. You may even begin to anticipate expected outcomes.

You perceive that many questions are repeated or adapted so that you can gain acute insights, which may enable you to score many sure points.

You learn how to confront new questions, or types of questions, and to attack them confidently and work out the correct answers.

You note objectives and emphases, and recognize pitfalls and dangers, so that you may make positive educational adjustments.

Moreover, you are kept fully informed in relation to new concepts, methods, practices, and directions in the field.

You discover that you are actually taking the examination all the time: you are preparing for the examination by "taking" an examination, not by reading extraneous and/or supererogatory textbooks.

In short, this PASSBOOK®, used directedly, should be an important factor in helping you to pass your test.

STATE OF NEW YORK
INSURANCE DEPARTMENT
AGENCY BUILDING ONE
THE GOVENOR NELSON A. ROCKEFELLER
EMPIRE STATE PLAZA
ALBANY, NEW YORK 12257

INFORMATION ON THE LICENSING OF BAIL BOND AGENTS

The licensing of bail bond insurance agents is regulated under Section 6802 of the New York State Insurance Law.

A prospective agent must pass a written examination before he may apply for a license. An outline of the examination is attached. A registration form for the examination is included in the enclosed handbook.

Insurance companies authorized to transact bail bond insurance in New York State supply the licensing application form to the prospective agent after he has passed the examination. This form must be completed by the applicant, affirmed by two persons who are able to vouch for him and returned to the company for endorsement. The application must be accompanied by two current photographs, a bond in the amount of $5,000 and a license fee. The licensing period is two years - from January 1 of odd years to December 31 of even years. Submit $50 with an individual application submitted in the first year of the period, $25 with an individual application submitted in the second year. Submit $50 per sub-licensee with a partnership, corporation or limited liability company application submitted in the first year of the period, $25 per sub-licensee with a partnership, corporation or limited liability company application submitted in the second year.*

If the applicant meets with tentative approval in the Licensing Bureau, the applicant will be notified to appear at the New York Office of the Insurance Department for an interview. Fingerprints will be taken for the Criminal Justice Services and Federal Bureau of Investigation and an investigation will be made through the court and police departments.

*Consult Insurance Department for latest fee information

OUTLINE OF EXAMINATIONS FOR APPLICANTS FOR
BAIL BOND LICENSES UNDER SECTION 6802 OF THE INSURANCE LAW

Underwriting, including the agent's responsibility to the public and to his company; preliminary investigation of the defendant's record. Knowledge of the jurisdiction and procedure of the criminal courts of New York State and political subdivisions of the State. The purpose and use of Bail Bonds.' Bail ;Bond forms, the Application and Indemnity Agreement, Bail Affidavit, Confession of Judgment, Consolidated Bail Bonds. The agent's Authority. Premiums. Definitions.

---

of the Criminal Procedure Law relevant to Bail Bonds, such as: Sections:

230.10	460.50	530.40	540.30
230.20	470.45	530.60	550.10
230.40	510.50	530.70	660.30
280.10	520.20	530.80	
330.50	530.20	540.10	
380.40 (1,2)	530.30	540.20	

Sections of Judiciary Law such as: 481

Sections of Penal Law such as: 10
   20
   175.45

Sections of the Insurance Law such as:

109	2122	2339
1214	2127	2604
2102	2309	6802
2117	2314	6804(a)
2120	2324	

Sections of the Vehicle & Traffic Law such as: 1808

HOW TO TAKE A TEST

I. YOU MUST PASS AN EXAMINATION

A. *WHAT EVERY CANDIDATE SHOULD KNOW*

Examination applicants often ask us for help in preparing for the written test. What can I study in advance? What kinds of questions will be asked? How will the test be given? How will the papers be graded?

As an applicant for a civil service examination, you may be wondering about some of these things. Our purpose here is to suggest effective methods of advance study and to describe civil service examinations.

Your chances for success on this examination can be increased if you know how to prepare. Those "pre-examination jitters" can be reduced if you know what to expect. You can even experience an adventure in good citizenship if you know why civil service exams are given.

B. *WHY ARE CIVIL SERVICE EXAMINATIONS GIVEN?*

Civil service examinations are important to you in two ways. As a citizen, you want public jobs filled by employees who know how to do their work. As a job seeker, you want a fair chance to compete for that job on an equal footing with other candidates. The best-known means of accomplishing this two-fold goal is the competitive examination.

Exams are widely publicized throughout the nation. They may be administered for jobs in federal, state, city, municipal, town or village governments or agencies.

Any citizen may apply, with some limitations, such as the age or residence of applicants. Your experience and education may be reviewed to see whether you meet the requirements for the particular examination. When these requirements exist, they are reasonable and applied consistently to all applicants. Thus, a competitive examination may cause you some uneasiness now, but it is your privilege and safeguard.

C. *HOW ARE CIVIL SERVICE EXAMS DEVELOPED?*

Examinations are carefully written by trained technicians who are specialists in the field known as "psychological measurement," in consultation with recognized authorities in the field of work that the test will cover. These experts recommend the subject matter areas or skills to be tested; only those knowledges or skills important to your success on the job are included. The most reliable books and source materials available are used as references. Together, the experts and technicians judge the difficulty level of the questions.

Test technicians know how to phrase questions so that the problem is clearly stated. Their ethics do not permit "trick" or "catch" questions. Questions may have been tried out on sample groups, or subjected to statistical analysis, to determine their usefulness.

Written tests are often used in combination with performance tests, ratings of training and experience, and oral interviews. All of these measures combine to form the best-known means of finding the right person for the right job.

II. HOW TO PASS THE WRITTEN TEST

A. *NATURE OF THE EXAMINATION*

To prepare intelligently for civil service examinations, you should know how they differ from school examinations you have taken. In school you were assigned certain definite pages to read or subjects to cover. The examination questions were quite detailed and usually emphasized memory. Civil service exams, on the other hand, try to discover your present ability to perform the duties of a position, plus your potentiality to learn these duties. In other words, a civil service exam attempts to predict how successful you will be. Questions cover such a broad area that they cannot be as minute and detailed as school exam questions.

In the public service similar kinds of work, or positions, are grouped together in one "class." This process is known as *position-classification*. All the positions in a class are paid according to the salary range for that class. One class title covers all of these positions, and they are all tested by the same examination.

B. *FOUR BASIC STEPS*

1) Study the announcement

How, then, can you know what subjects to study? Our best answer is: "Learn as much as possible about the class of positions for which you've applied." The exam will test the knowledge, skills and abilities needed to do the work.

Your most valuable source of information about the position you want is the official exam announcement. This announcement lists the training and experience qualifications. Check these standards and apply only if you come reasonably close to meeting them.

The brief description of the position in the examination announcement offers some clues to the subjects which will be tested. Think about the job itself. Review the duties in your mind. Can you perform them, or are there some in which you are rusty? Fill in the blank spots in your preparation.

Many jurisdictions preview the written test in the exam announcement by including a section called "Knowledge and Abilities Required," "Scope of the Examination," or some similar heading. Here you will find out specifically what fields will be tested.

2) Review your own background

Once you learn in general what the position is all about, and what you need to know to do the work, ask yourself which subjects you already know fairly well and which need improvement. You may wonder whether to concentrate on improving your strong areas or on building some background in your fields of weakness. When the announcement has specified "some knowledge" or "considerable knowledge," or has used adjectives like "beginning principles of…" or "advanced … methods," you can get a clue as to the number and difficulty of questions to be asked in any given field. More questions, and hence broader coverage, would be included for those subjects which are more important in the work. Now weigh your strengths and weaknesses against the job requirements and prepare accordingly.

3) Determine the level of the position

Another way to tell how intensively you should prepare is to understand the level of the job for which you are applying. Is it the entering level? In other words, is this the position in which beginners in a field of work are hired? Or is it an intermediate or advanced level? Sometimes this is indicated by such words as "Junior" or "Senior" in the class title. Other jurisdictions use Roman numerals to designate the level – Clerk I, Clerk II, for example. The word "Supervisor" sometimes appears in the title. If the level is not indicated by the title, check the description of duties. Will you be working under very close supervision, or will you have responsibility for independent decisions in this work?

4) Choose appropriate study materials

Now that you know the subjects to be examined and the relative amount of each subject to be covered, you can choose suitable study materials. For beginning level jobs, or even advanced ones, if you have a pronounced weakness in some aspect of your training, read a modern, standard textbook in that field. Be sure it is up to date and has general coverage. Such books are normally available at your library, and the librarian will be glad to help you locate one. For entry-level positions, questions of appropriate difficulty are chosen – neither highly advanced questions, nor those too simple. Such questions require careful thought but not advanced training.

If the position for which you are applying is technical or advanced, you will read more advanced, specialized material. If you are already familiar with the basic principles of your field, elementary textbooks would waste your time. Concentrate on advanced textbooks and technical periodicals. Think through the concepts and review difficult problems in your field.

These are all general sources. You can get more ideas on your own initiative, following these leads. For example, training manuals and publications of the government agency which employs workers in your field can be useful, particularly for technical and professional positions. A letter or visit to the government department involved may result in more specific study suggestions, and certainly will provide you with a more definite idea of the exact nature of the position you are seeking.

III. KINDS OF TESTS

Tests are used for purposes other than measuring knowledge and ability to perform specified duties. For some positions, it is equally important to test ability to make adjustments to new situations or to profit from training. In others, basic mental abilities not dependent on information are essential. Questions which test these things may not appear as pertinent to the duties of the position as those which test for knowledge and information. Yet they are often highly important parts of a fair examination. For very general questions, it is almost impossible to help you direct your study efforts. What we can do is to point out some of the more common of these general abilities needed in public service positions and describe some typical questions.

1) General information

Broad, general information has been found useful for predicting job success in some kinds of work. This is tested in a variety of ways, from vocabulary lists to questions about current events. Basic background in some field of work, such as sociology or economics, may be sampled in a group of questions. Often these are principles which have become familiar to most persons through exposure rather than through formal training. It is difficult to advise you how to study for these questions; being alert to the world around you is our best suggestion.

2) Verbal ability

An example of an ability needed in many positions is verbal or language ability. Verbal ability is, in brief, the ability to use and understand words. Vocabulary and grammar tests are typical measures of this ability. Reading comprehension or paragraph interpretation questions are common in many kinds of civil service tests. You are given a paragraph of written material and asked to find its central meaning.

3) Numerical ability

Number skills can be tested by the familiar arithmetic problem, by checking paired lists of numbers to see which are alike and which are different, or by interpreting charts and graphs. In the latter test, a graph may be printed in the test booklet which you are asked to use as the basis for answering questions.

4) Observation

A popular test for law-enforcement positions is the observation test. A picture is shown to you for several minutes, then taken away. Questions about the picture test your ability to observe both details and larger elements.

5) Following directions

In many positions in the public service, the employee must be able to carry out written instructions dependably and accurately. You may be given a chart with several columns, each column listing a variety of information. The questions require you to carry out directions involving the information given in the chart.

6) Skills and aptitudes

Performance tests effectively measure some manual skills and aptitudes. When the skill is one in which you are trained, such as typing or shorthand, you can practice. These tests are often very much like those given in business school or high school courses. For many of the other skills and aptitudes, however, no short-time preparation can be made. Skills and abilities natural to you or that you have developed throughout your lifetime are being tested.

Many of the general questions just described provide all the data needed to answer the questions and ask you to use your reasoning ability to find the answers. Your best preparation for these tests, as well as for tests of facts and ideas, is to be at your physical and mental best. You, no doubt, have your own methods of getting into an exam-taking mood and keeping "in shape." The next section lists some ideas on this subject.

IV. KINDS OF QUESTIONS

Only rarely is the "essay" question, which you answer in narrative form, used in civil service tests. Civil service tests are usually of the short-answer type. Full instructions for answering these questions will be given to you at the examination. But in case this is your first experience with short-answer questions and separate answer sheets, here is what you need to know:

1) **Multiple-choice Questions**

Most popular of the short-answer questions is the "multiple choice" or "best answer" question. It can be used, for example, to test for factual knowledge, ability to solve problems or judgment in meeting situations found at work.

A multiple-choice question is normally one of three types—
- It can begin with an incomplete statement followed by several possible endings. You are to find the one ending which *best* completes the statement, although some of the others may not be entirely wrong.
- It can also be a complete statement in the form of a question which is answered by choosing one of the statements listed.

- It can be in the form of a problem – again you select the best answer.

Here is an example of a multiple-choice question with a discussion which should give you some clues as to the method for choosing the right answer:

When an employee has a complaint about his assignment, the action which will *best* help him overcome his difficulty is to
- A. discuss his difficulty with his coworkers
- B. take the problem to the head of the organization
- C. take the problem to the person who gave him the assignment
- D. say nothing to anyone about his complaint

In answering this question, you should study each of the choices to find which is best. Consider choice "A" – Certainly an employee may discuss his complaint with fellow employees, but no change or improvement can result, and the complaint remains unresolved. Choice "B" is a poor choice since the head of the organization probably does not know what assignment you have been given, and taking your problem to him is known as "going over the head" of the supervisor. The supervisor, or person who made the assignment, is the person who can clarify it or correct any injustice. Choice "C" is, therefore, correct. To say nothing, as in choice "D," is unwise. Supervisors have and interest in knowing the problems employees are facing, and the employee is seeking a solution to his problem.

2) True/False Questions

The "true/false" or "right/wrong" form of question is sometimes used. Here a complete statement is given. Your job is to decide whether the statement is right or wrong.

SAMPLE: A roaming cell-phone call to a nearby city costs less than a non-roaming call to a distant city.

This statement is wrong, or false, since roaming calls are more expensive.

This is not a complete list of all possible question forms, although most of the others are variations of these common types. You will always get complete directions for answering questions. Be sure you understand *how* to mark your answers – ask questions until you do.

V. RECORDING YOUR ANSWERS

Computer terminals are used more and more today for many different kinds of exams.

For an examination with very few applicants, you may be told to record your answers in the test booklet itself. Separate answer sheets are much more common. If this separate answer sheet is to be scored by machine – and this is often the case – it is highly important that you mark your answers correctly in order to get credit.

An electronic scoring machine is often used in civil service offices because of the speed with which papers can be scored. Machine-scored answer sheets must be marked with a pencil, which will be given to you. This pencil has a high graphite content which responds to the electronic scoring machine. As a matter of fact, stray dots may register as answers, so do not let your pencil rest on the answer sheet while you are pondering the correct answer. Also, if your pencil lead breaks or is otherwise defective, ask for another.

Since the answer sheet will be dropped in a slot in the scoring machine, be careful not to bend the corners or get the paper crumpled.

The answer sheet normally has five vertical columns of numbers, with 30 numbers to a column. These numbers correspond to the question numbers in your test booklet. After each number, going across the page are four or five pairs of dotted lines. These short dotted lines have small letters or numbers above them. The first two pairs may also have a "T" or "F" above the letters. This indicates that the first two pairs only are to be used if the questions are of the true-false type. If the questions are multiple choice, disregard the "T" and "F" and pay attention only to the small letters or numbers.

Answer your questions in the manner of the sample that follows:

32. The largest city in the United States is
   A. Washington, D.C.
   B. New York City
   C. Chicago
   D. Detroit
   E. San Francisco

1) Choose the answer you think is best. (New York City is the largest, so "B" is correct.)
2) Find the row of dotted lines numbered the same as the question you are answering. (Find row number 32)
3) Find the pair of dotted lines corresponding to the answer. (Find the pair of lines under the mark "B.")
4) Make a solid black mark between the dotted lines.

VI. BEFORE THE TEST

Common sense will help you find procedures to follow to get ready for an examination. Too many of us, however, overlook these sensible measures. Indeed, nervousness and fatigue have been found to be the most serious reasons why applicants fail to do their best on civil service tests. Here is a list of reminders:

- Begin your preparation early – Don't wait until the last minute to go scurrying around for books and materials or to find out what the position is all about.
- Prepare continuously – An hour a night for a week is better than an all-night cram session. This has been definitely established. What is more, a night a week for a month will return better dividends than crowding your study into a shorter period of time.
- Locate the place of the exam – You have been sent a notice telling you when and where to report for the examination. If the location is in a different town or otherwise unfamiliar to you, it would be well to inquire the best route and learn something about the building.
- Relax the night before the test – Allow your mind to rest. Do not study at all that night. Plan some mild recreation or diversion; then go to bed early and get a good night's sleep.
- Get up early enough to make a leisurely trip to the place for the test – This way unforeseen events, traffic snarls, unfamiliar buildings, etc. will not upset you.
- Dress comfortably – A written test is not a fashion show. You will be known by number and not by name, so wear something comfortable.

- Leave excess paraphernalia at home – Shopping bags and odd bundles will get in your way. You need bring only the items mentioned in the official notice you received; usually everything you need is provided. Do not bring reference books to the exam. They will only confuse those last minutes and be taken away from you when in the test room.
- Arrive somewhat ahead of time – If because of transportation schedules you must get there very early, bring a newspaper or magazine to take your mind off yourself while waiting.
- Locate the examination room – When you have found the proper room, you will be directed to the seat or part of the room where you will sit. Sometimes you are given a sheet of instructions to read while you are waiting. Do not fill out any forms until you are told to do so; just read them and be prepared.
- Relax and prepare to listen to the instructions
- If you have any physical problem that may keep you from doing your best, be sure to tell the test administrator. If you are sick or in poor health, you really cannot do your best on the exam. You can come back and take the test some other time.

VII. AT THE TEST

The day of the test is here and you have the test booklet in your hand. The temptation to get going is very strong. Caution! There is more to success than knowing the right answers. You must know how to identify your papers and understand variations in the type of short-answer question used in this particular examination. Follow these suggestions for maximum results from your efforts:

1) Cooperate with the monitor

The test administrator has a duty to create a situation in which you can be as much at ease as possible. He will give instructions, tell you when to begin, check to see that you are marking your answer sheet correctly, and so on. He is not there to guard you, although he will see that your competitors do not take unfair advantage. He wants to help you do your best.

2) Listen to all instructions

Don't jump the gun! Wait until you understand all directions. In most civil service tests you get more time than you need to answer the questions. So don't be in a hurry. Read each word of instructions until you clearly understand the meaning. Study the examples, listen to all announcements and follow directions. Ask questions if you do not understand what to do.

3) Identify your papers

Civil service exams are usually identified by number only. You will be assigned a number; you must not put your name on your test papers. Be sure to copy your number correctly. Since more than one exam may be given, copy your exact examination title.

4) Plan your time

Unless you are told that a test is a "speed" or "rate of work" test, speed itself is usually not important. Time enough to answer all the questions will be provided, but this does not mean that you have all day. An overall time limit has been set. Divide the total time (in minutes) by the number of questions to determine the approximate time you have for each question.

5) Do not linger over difficult questions

If you come across a difficult question, mark it with a paper clip (useful to have along) and come back to it when you have been through the booklet. One caution if you do this – be sure to skip a number on your answer sheet as well. Check often to be sure that you have not lost your place and that you are marking in the row numbered the same as the question you are answering.

6) Read the questions

Be sure you know what the question asks! Many capable people are unsuccessful because they failed to *read* the questions correctly.

7) Answer all questions

Unless you have been instructed that a penalty will be deducted for incorrect answers, it is better to guess than to omit a question.

8) Speed tests

It is often better NOT to guess on speed tests. It has been found that on timed tests people are tempted to spend the last few seconds before time is called in marking answers at random – without even reading them – in the hope of picking up a few extra points. To discourage this practice, the instructions may warn you that your score will be "corrected" for guessing. That is, a penalty will be applied. The incorrect answers will be deducted from the correct ones, or some other penalty formula will be used.

9) Review your answers

If you finish before time is called, go back to the questions you guessed or omitted to give them further thought. Review other answers if you have time.

10) Return your test materials

If you are ready to leave before others have finished or time is called, take ALL your materials to the monitor and leave quietly. Never take any test material with you. The monitor can discover whose papers are not complete, and taking a test booklet may be grounds for disqualification.

VIII. EXAMINATION TECHNIQUES

1) Read the general instructions carefully. These are usually printed on the first page of the exam booklet. As a rule, these instructions refer to the timing of the examination; the fact that you should not start work until the signal and must stop work at a signal, etc. If there are any *special* instructions, such as a choice of questions to be answered, make sure that you note this instruction carefully.

2) When you are ready to start work on the examination, that is as soon as the signal has been given, read the instructions to each question booklet, underline any key words or phrases, such as *least, best, outline, describe* and the like. In this way you will tend to answer as requested rather than discover on reviewing your paper that you *listed without describing*, that you selected the *worst* choice rather than the *best* choice, etc.

3) If the examination is of the objective or multiple-choice type – that is, each question will also give a series of possible answers: A, B, C or D, and you are called upon to select the best answer and write the letter next to that answer on your answer paper – it is advisable to start answering each question in turn. There may be anywhere from 50 to 100 such questions in the three or four hours allotted and you can see how much time would be taken if you read through all the questions before beginning to answer any. Furthermore, if you come across a question or group of questions which you know would be difficult to answer, it would undoubtedly affect your handling of all the other questions.

4) If the examination is of the essay type and contains but a few questions, it is a moot point as to whether you should read all the questions before starting to answer any one. Of course, if you are given a choice – say five out of seven and the like – then it is essential to read all the questions so you can eliminate the two that are most difficult. If, however, you are asked to answer all the questions, there may be danger in trying to answer the easiest one first because you may find that you will spend too much time on it. The best technique is to answer the first question, then proceed to the second, etc.

5) Time your answers. Before the exam begins, write down the time it started, then add the time allowed for the examination and write down the time it must be completed, then divide the time available somewhat as follows:
    - If 3-1/2 hours are allowed, that would be 210 minutes. If you have 80 objective-type questions, that would be an average of 2-1/2 minutes per question. Allow yourself no more than 2 minutes per question, or a total of 160 minutes, which will permit about 50 minutes to review.
    - If for the time allotment of 210 minutes there are 7 essay questions to answer, that would average about 30 minutes a question. Give yourself only 25 minutes per question so that you have about 35 minutes to review.

6) The most important instruction is to *read each question* and make sure you know what is wanted. The second most important instruction is to *time yourself properly* so that you answer every question. The third most important instruction is to *answer every question*. Guess if you have to but include something for each question. Remember that you will receive no credit for a blank and will probably receive some credit if you write something in answer to an essay question. If you guess a letter – say "B" for a multiple-choice question – you may have guessed right. If you leave a blank as an answer to a multiple-choice question, the examiners may respect your feelings but it will not add a point to your score. Some exams may penalize you for wrong answers, so in such cases *only*, you may not want to guess unless you have some basis for your answer.

7) Suggestions
    a. Objective-type questions
        1. Examine the question booklet for proper sequence of pages and questions
        2. Read all instructions carefully
        3. Skip any question which seems too difficult; return to it after all other questions have been answered
        4. Apportion your time properly; do not spend too much time on any single question or group of questions

5. Note and underline key words – *all, most, fewest, least, best, worst, same, opposite,* etc.
6. Pay particular attention to negatives
7. Note unusual option, e.g., unduly long, short, complex, different or similar in content to the body of the question
8. Observe the use of "hedging" words – *probably, may, most likely,* etc.
9. Make sure that your answer is put next to the same number as the question
10. Do not second-guess unless you have good reason to believe the second answer is definitely more correct
11. Cross out original answer if you decide another answer is more accurate; do not erase until you are ready to hand your paper in
12. Answer all questions; guess unless instructed otherwise
13. Leave time for review

   b. Essay questions
   1. Read each question carefully
   2. Determine exactly what is wanted. Underline key words or phrases.
   3. Decide on outline or paragraph answer
   4. Include many different points and elements unless asked to develop any one or two points or elements
   5. Show impartiality by giving pros and cons unless directed to select one side only
   6. Make and write down any assumptions you find necessary to answer the questions
   7. Watch your English, grammar, punctuation and choice of words
   8. Time your answers; don't crowd material

8) Answering the essay question

Most essay questions can be answered by framing the specific response around several key words or ideas. Here are a few such key words or ideas:

M's: manpower, materials, methods, money, management
P's: purpose, program, policy, plan, procedure, practice, problems, pitfalls, personnel, public relations

   a. Six basic steps in handling problems:
   1. Preliminary plan and background development
   2. Collect information, data and facts
   3. Analyze and interpret information, data and facts
   4. Analyze and develop solutions as well as make recommendations
   5. Prepare report and sell recommendations
   6. Install recommendations and follow up effectiveness

   b. Pitfalls to avoid
   1. *Taking things for granted* – A statement of the situation does not necessarily imply that each of the elements is necessarily true; for example, a complaint may be invalid and biased so that all that can be taken for granted is that a complaint has been registered

2. *Considering only one side of a situation* – Wherever possible, indicate several alternatives and then point out the reasons you selected the best one
3. *Failing to indicate follow up* – Whenever your answer indicates action on your part, make certain that you will take proper follow-up action to see how successful your recommendations, procedures or actions turn out to be
4. *Taking too long in answering any single question* – Remember to time your answers properly

IX. AFTER THE TEST

Scoring procedures differ in detail among civil service jurisdictions although the general principles are the same. Whether the papers are hand-scored or graded by machine we have described, they are nearly always graded by number. That is, the person who marks the paper knows only the number – never the name – of the applicant. Not until all the papers have been graded will they be matched with names. If other tests, such as training and experience or oral interview ratings have been given, scores will be combined. Different parts of the examination usually have different weights. For example, the written test might count 60 percent of the final grade, and a rating of training and experience 40 percent. In many jurisdictions, veterans will have a certain number of points added to their grades.

After the final grade has been determined, the names are placed in grade order and an eligible list is established. There are various methods for resolving ties between those who get the same final grade – probably the most common is to place first the name of the person whose application was received first. Job offers are made from the eligible list in the order the names appear on it. You will be notified of your grade and your rank as soon as all these computations have been made. This will be done as rapidly as possible.

People who are found to meet the requirements in the announcement are called "eligibles." Their names are put on a list of eligible candidates. An eligible's chances of getting a job depend on how high he stands on this list and how fast agencies are filling jobs from the list.

When a job is to be filled from a list of eligibles, the agency asks for the names of people on the list of eligibles for that job. When the civil service commission receives this request, it sends to the agency the names of the three people highest on this list. Or, if the job to be filled has specialized requirements, the office sends the agency the names of the top three persons who meet these requirements from the general list.

The appointing officer makes a choice from among the three people whose names were sent to him. If the selected person accepts the appointment, the names of the others are put back on the list to be considered for future openings.

That is the rule in hiring from all kinds of eligible lists, whether they are for typist, carpenter, chemist, or something else. For every vacancy, the appointing officer has his choice of any one of the top three eligibles on the list. This explains why the person whose name is on top of the list sometimes does not get an appointment when some of the persons lower on the list do. If the appointing officer chooses the second or third eligible, the No. 1 eligible does not get a job at once, but stays on the list until he is appointed or the list is terminated.

X. HOW TO PASS THE INTERVIEW TEST

The examination for which you applied requires an oral interview test. You have already taken the written test and you are now being called for the interview test – the final part of the formal examination.

You may think that it is not possible to prepare for an interview test and that there are no procedures to follow during an interview. Our purpose is to point out some things you can do in advance that will help you and some good rules to follow and pitfalls to avoid while you are being interviewed.

What is an interview supposed to test?

The written examination is designed to test the technical knowledge and competence of the candidate; the oral is designed to evaluate intangible qualities, not readily measured otherwise, and to establish a list showing the relative fitness of each candidate – as measured against his competitors – for the position sought. Scoring is not on the basis of "right" and "wrong," but on a sliding scale of values ranging from "not passable" to "outstanding." As a matter of fact, it is possible to achieve a relatively low score without a single "incorrect" answer because of evident weakness in the qualities being measured.

Occasionally, an examination may consist entirely of an oral test – either an individual or a group oral. In such cases, information is sought concerning the technical knowledges and abilities of the candidate, since there has been no written examination for this purpose. More commonly, however, an oral test is used to supplement a written examination.

Who conducts interviews?

The composition of oral boards varies among different jurisdictions. In nearly all, a representative of the personnel department serves as chairman. One of the members of the board may be a representative of the department in which the candidate would work. In some cases, "outside experts" are used, and, frequently, a businessman or some other representative of the general public is asked to serve. Labor and management or other special groups may be represented. The aim is to secure the services of experts in the appropriate field.

However the board is composed, it is a good idea (and not at all improper or unethical) to ascertain in advance of the interview who the members are and what groups they represent. When you are introduced to them, you will have some idea of their backgrounds and interests, and at least you will not stutter and stammer over their names.

What should be done before the interview?

While knowledge about the board members is useful and takes some of the surprise element out of the interview, there is other preparation which is more substantive. It *is* possible to prepare for an oral interview – in several ways:

1) Keep a copy of your application and review it carefully before the interview

This may be the only document before the oral board, and the starting point of the interview. Know what education and experience you have listed there, and the sequence and dates of all of it. Sometimes the board will ask you to review the highlights of your experience for them; you should not have to hem and haw doing it.

2) Study the class specification and the examination announcement

Usually, the oral board has one or both of these to guide them. The qualities, characteristics or knowledges required by the position sought are stated in these documents. They offer valuable clues as to the nature of the oral interview. For example, if the job involves supervisory responsibilities, the announcement will usually indicate that knowledge of modern supervisory methods and the qualifications of the candidate as a supervisor will be tested. If so, you can expect such questions, frequently in the form of a hypothetical situation which you are expected to solve. NEVER go into an oral without knowledge of the duties and responsibilities of the job you seek.

3) Think through each qualification required

Try to visualize the kind of questions you would ask if you were a board member. How well could you answer them? Try especially to appraise your own knowledge and background in each area, *measured against the job sought*, and identify any areas in which you are weak. Be critical and realistic – do not flatter yourself.

4) Do some general reading in areas in which you feel you may be weak

For example, if the job involves supervision and your past experience has NOT, some general reading in supervisory methods and practices, particularly in the field of human relations, might be useful. Do NOT study agency procedures or detailed manuals. The oral board will be testing your understanding and capacity, not your memory.

5) Get a good night's sleep and watch your general health and mental attitude

You will want a clear head at the interview. Take care of a cold or any other minor ailment, and of course, no hangovers.

What should be done on the day of the interview?

Now comes the day of the interview itself. Give yourself plenty of time to get there. Plan to arrive somewhat ahead of the scheduled time, particularly if your appointment is in the fore part of the day. If a previous candidate fails to appear, the board might be ready for you a bit early. By early afternoon an oral board is almost invariably behind schedule if there are many candidates, and you may have to wait. Take along a book or magazine to read, or your application to review, but leave any extraneous material in the waiting room when you go in for your interview. In any event, relax and compose yourself.

The matter of dress is important. The board is forming impressions about you – from your experience, your manners, your attitude, and your appearance. Give your personal appearance careful attention. Dress your best, but not your flashiest. Choose conservative, appropriate clothing, and be sure it is immaculate. This is a business interview, and your appearance should indicate that you regard it as such. Besides, being well groomed and properly dressed will help boost your confidence.

Sooner or later, someone will call your name and escort you into the interview room. *This is it.* From here on you are on your own. It is too late for any more preparation. But remember, you asked for this opportunity to prove your fitness, and you are here because your request was granted.

What happens when you go in?

The usual sequence of events will be as follows: The clerk (who is often the board stenographer) will introduce you to the chairman of the oral board, who will introduce you to the other members of the board. Acknowledge the introductions before you sit down. Do not be surprised if you find a microphone facing you or a stenotypist sitting by. Oral interviews are usually recorded in the event of an appeal or other review.

Usually the chairman of the board will open the interview by reviewing the highlights of your education and work experience from your application – primarily for the benefit of the other members of the board, as well as to get the material into the record. Do not interrupt or comment unless there is an error or significant misinterpretation; if that is the case, do not hesitate. But do not quibble about insignificant matters. Also, he will usually ask you some question about your education, experience or your present job – partly to get you to start talking and to establish the interviewing "rapport." He may start the actual questioning, or turn it over to one of the other members. Frequently, each member undertakes the questioning on a particular area, one in which he is perhaps most competent, so you can expect each member to participate in the examination. Because time is limited, you may also expect some rather abrupt switches in the direction the questioning takes, so do not be upset by it. Normally, a board member will not pursue a single line of questioning unless he discovers a particular strength or weakness.

After each member has participated, the chairman will usually ask whether any member has any further questions, then will ask you if you have anything you wish to add. Unless you are expecting this question, it may floor you. Worse, it may start you off on an extended, extemporaneous speech. The board is not usually seeking more information. The question is principally to offer you a last opportunity to present further qualifications or to indicate that you have nothing to add. So, if you feel that a significant qualification or characteristic has been overlooked, it is proper to point it out in a sentence or so. Do not compliment the board on the thoroughness of their examination – they have been sketchy, and you know it. If you wish, merely say, "No thank you, I have nothing further to add." This is a point where you can "talk yourself out" of a good impression or fail to present an important bit of information. Remember, *you close the interview yourself*.

The chairman will then say, "That is all, Mr. _____, thank you." Do not be startled; the interview is over, and quicker than you think. Thank him, gather your belongings and take your leave. Save your sigh of relief for the other side of the door.

How to put your best foot forward

Throughout this entire process, you may feel that the board individually and collectively is trying to pierce your defenses, seek out your hidden weaknesses and embarrass and confuse you. Actually, this is not true. They are obliged to make an appraisal of your qualifications for the job you are seeking, and they want to see you in your best light. Remember, they must interview all candidates and a non-cooperative candidate may become a failure in spite of their best efforts to bring out his qualifications. Here are 15 suggestions that will help you:

1) Be natural – Keep your attitude confident, not cocky

If you are not confident that you can do the job, do not expect the board to be. Do not apologize for your weaknesses, try to bring out your strong points. The board is interested in a positive, not negative, presentation. Cockiness will antagonize any board member and make him wonder if you are covering up a weakness by a false show of strength.

2) Get comfortable, but don't lounge or sprawl

Sit erectly but not stiffly. A careless posture may lead the board to conclude that you are careless in other things, or at least that you are not impressed by the importance of the occasion. Either conclusion is natural, even if incorrect. Do not fuss with your clothing, a pencil or an ashtray. Your hands may occasionally be useful to emphasize a point; do not let them become a point of distraction.

3) Do not wisecrack or make small talk

This is a serious situation, and your attitude should show that you consider it as such. Further, the time of the board is limited – they do not want to waste it, and neither should you.

4) Do not exaggerate your experience or abilities
In the first place, from information in the application or other interviews and sources, the board may know more about you than you think. Secondly, you probably will not get away with it. An experienced board is rather adept at spotting such a situation, so do not take the chance.

5) If you know a board member, do not make a point of it, yet do not hide it
Certainly you are not fooling him, and probably not the other members of the board. Do not try to take advantage of your acquaintanceship – it will probably do you little good.

6) Do not dominate the interview
Let the board do that. They will give you the clues – do not assume that you have to do all the talking. Realize that the board has a number of questions to ask you, and do not try to take up all the interview time by showing off your extensive knowledge of the answer to the first one.

7) Be attentive
You only have 20 minutes or so, and you should keep your attention at its sharpest throughout. When a member is addressing a problem or question to you, give him your undivided attention. Address your reply principally to him, but do not exclude the other board members.

8) Do not interrupt
A board member may be stating a problem for you to analyze. He will ask you a question when the time comes. Let him state the problem, and wait for the question.

9) Make sure you understand the question
Do not try to answer until you are sure what the question is. If it is not clear, restate it in your own words or ask the board member to clarify it for you. However, do not haggle about minor elements.

10) Reply promptly but not hastily
A common entry on oral board rating sheets is "candidate responded readily," or "candidate hesitated in replies." Respond as promptly and quickly as you can, but do not jump to a hasty, ill-considered answer.

11) Do not be peremptory in your answers
A brief answer is proper – but do not fire your answer back. That is a losing game from your point of view. The board member can probably ask questions much faster than you can answer them.

12) Do not try to create the answer you think the board member wants
He is interested in what kind of mind you have and how it works – not in playing games. Furthermore, he can usually spot this practice and will actually grade you down on it.

13) Do not switch sides in your reply merely to agree with a board member
Frequently, a member will take a contrary position merely to draw you out and to see if you are willing and able to defend your point of view. Do not start a debate, yet do not surrender a good position. If a position is worth taking, it is worth defending.

14) Do not be afraid to admit an error in judgment if you are shown to be wrong

The board knows that you are forced to reply without any opportunity for careful consideration. Your answer may be demonstrably wrong. If so, admit it and get on with the interview.

15) Do not dwell at length on your present job

The opening question may relate to your present assignment. Answer the question but do not go into an extended discussion. You are being examined for a *new* job, not your present one. As a matter of fact, try to phrase ALL your answers in terms of the job for which you are being examined.

Basis of Rating

Probably you will forget most of these "do's" and "don'ts" when you walk into the oral interview room. Even remembering them all will not ensure you a passing grade. Perhaps you did not have the qualifications in the first place. But remembering them will help you to put your best foot forward, without treading on the toes of the board members.

Rumor and popular opinion to the contrary notwithstanding, an oral board wants you to make the best appearance possible. They know you are under pressure – but they also want to see how you respond to it as a guide to what your reaction would be under the pressures of the job you seek. They will be influenced by the degree of poise you display, the personal traits you show and the manner in which you respond.

ABOUT THIS BOOK

This book contains tests divided into Examination Sections. Go through each test, answering every question in the margin. We have also attached a sample answer sheet at the back of the book that can be removed and used. At the end of each test look at the answer key and check your answers. On the ones you got wrong, look at the right answer choice and learn. Do not fill in the answers first. Do not memorize the questions and answers, but understand the answer and principles involved. On your test, the questions will likely be different from the samples. Questions are changed and new ones added. If you understand these past questions you should have success with any changes that arise. Tests may consist of several types of questions. We have additional books on each subject should more study be advisable or necessary for you. Finally, the more you study, the better prepared you will be. This book is intended to be the last thing you study before you walk into the examination room. Prior study of relevant texts is also recommended. NLC publishes some of these in our Fundamental Series. Knowledge and good sense are important factors in passing your exam. Good luck also helps. So now study this Passbook, absorb the material contained within and take that knowledge into the examination. Then do your best to pass that exam.

EXAMINATION SECTION

EXAMINATION SECTION
TEST 1

DIRECTIONS: Each question or incomplete statement is followed by several suggested answers or completions. Select the one that BEST answers the question or completes the statement. *PRINT THE LETTER OF THE CORRECT ANSWER IN THE SPACE AT THE RIGHT.*

1. A _____ bond is a guarantee that a contractor will enter into a contract if it is awarded to him.

    A. bid
    B. surety
    C. fidelity
    D. named schedule

    1.____

2. A bail agent may often have to check on the status of a signer's deed to real property if the property has been offered as collateral on a bond. In public records, the most common type of deed is the _____ deed.

    A. fee simple
    B. quitclaim
    C. freehold
    D. warranty

    2.____

3. A bondsman's reserve account is ordinarily established by

    A. the bondsman himself
    B. the surety company
    C. individual signers
    D. the local municipality

    3.____

4. What is the term for the person whose obligation is guaranteed by a bond?

    A. Obligee   B. Bailee   C. Arrestee   D. Principal

    4.____

5. An agent's main concern in writing a bond is generally

    A. presenting a convincing argument to the court
    B. securing prompt payment of the premium
    C. negotiating the highest premium possible
    D. being able to recover if the bail is forfeited

    5.____

6. An agent is checking the deed of a signer's property which has been offered as collateral on a bond. Which of the following forms of estate would make for the strongest collateral?

    A. Leasehold
    B. Fee simple
    C. Leased fee
    D. Life estate

    6.____

7. When talking with a potential signer about writing a bond, what is the first question that should be asked?

    A. What was the offense?
    B. Is the defendant employed?
    C. What is being offered as collateral?
    D. When was the defendant arrested?

    7.____

1

8. A *bailee* is

   A. the individual appointed by an insurance company to solicit, negotiate, effect or countersign bail agreements on its behalf
   B. a person in custody whose release may be secured by posting bail
   C. a person or concern having possession of property committed in trust from the owner
   D. the person protected by the bail bond

9. Which of the following items of information typically appears FIRST on an application for bail?

   A. Information on defendant
   B. Booking information
   C. Information on defendant's family
   D. Information on signer

10. An arrangement whereby one party becomes answerable to a third party for the acts of a second party is known as a

    A. trust   B. deed
    C. surety   D. power of attorney

11. In terms of the defendant, the bail bond agent's main concern in bailing him or her out of jail is that

    A. the defendant be present for all scheduled court appearances
    B. there is a reasonable likelihood that the defendant is innocent of the charges
    C. the defendant offers genuine remorse for what he or she has done
    D. the defendant will plead the case out quickly

12. A piece of real property is being used as collateral on a bond. Who must sign the bail agreement?

    A. The defendant and the person whose name appears on the deed
    B. The defendant, the person whose name appears on the deed, and anyone currently leasing the property
    C. Only the person whose name appears on the deed
    D. Only the defendant

13. In the case of a bail skip, a bounty hunter's fees are typically paid by the

    A. bail bond agent   B. defendant
    C. surety company   D. signer

14. An obligation of an insurance company against financial loss caused by the dishonest acts of its employees or agents is a

    A. surety bond   B. fidelity bond
    C. performance bond   D. trust

15. A signer to a deed has no substantial property assets to offer for collateral on a bond. If the agent requires only the signer's signature along with some cash as collateral, the agent's main concern should be the

    A. employment history of the defendant
    B. seriousness of the offense for which the defendant is accused
    C. employment history of the signer
    D. arrest record of the signer

16. Most bondsmen prefer _____ as collateral on a bond.

    A. jewelry   B. real estate
    C. automobiles   D. cash

17. Which of the following cases would probably require the strongest collateral for a bond?

    A. A 40-year-old arrested on forgery charges
    B. A 14-year-old arrested for vandalism
    C. An 18-year-old arrested for a robbery in which a gun was used
    D. A 45-year-old parent arrested on kidnapping charges for abducting a son or daughter from the estranged spouse

18. Which of the following is NOT a term for the signer of a bail bond?

    A. Obligor   B. Trustee
    C. Principal   D. Indemnitor

19. In general, a period of _____ hours is the maximum limit for a court to bring an arrestee before a judicial officer.

    A. 6   B. 12   C. 24   D. 48

20. In tracking a bail skip, the agent's first step should usually be to

    A. check the jails   B. hire a bounty hunter
    C. contact the police   D. contact the signer

21. In most cases, real property is deeded to the state if taxes have not been paid for a period of at LEAST _____ year(s).

    A. 1   B. 3   C. 5   D. 10

22. Which of the following forms is used to inform the signer of his or her obligation to a bondsman and the insurance company?

    A. Face sheet   B. Power of attorney
    C. Application for bail   D. Bail agreement

23. Probably the best way to determine the risk of a defendant in terms of writing a bond is to look at the

    A. seriousness of the offense
    B. quality of collateral on the bond
    C. defendant's employment history
    D. amount of bail

24. The most effective way for an agent to handle a past due account is to

    A. send a threatening letter regarding foreclosure or garnishment
    B. leave the client alone for a few days, and then attempt to work out a payment plan
    C. initiate punitive measures such as foreclosure or garnishment without notifying the signer
    D. contact the surety company to initiate subrogation

25. A piece of real property has been offered as collateral on a bond. A check of the deed reveals that the property is jointly owned by 3 siblings. In order to be valid, the bond must at the very least be signed by

    A. the eldest of the siblings
    B. the sibling who acted as executor when the property was conveyed
    C. two of the three siblings
    D. all three of the siblings who own the property

KEY (CORRECT ANSWERS)

1. A
2. B
3. B
4. D
5. D

6. B
7. D
8. C
9. B
10. C

11. A
12. C
13. D
14. B
15. C

16. B
17. C
18. B
19. A
20. D

21. C
22. D
23. C
24. B
25. D

TEST 2

DIRECTIONS: Each question or incomplete statement is followed by several suggested answers or completions. Select the one that BEST answers the question or completes the statement. *PRINT THE LETTER OF THE CORRECT ANSWER IN THE SPACE AT THE RIGHT.*

1. What is the term for the seizing of a criminal defendant's property?

    A. Arrogation B. Impoundment
    C. Attachment D. Snatch

2. In surety bonds, the person protected by the bond is known as the

    A. principal B. obligor C. bailee D. obligee

3. The primary purpose of a bondsman's reserve account should be to

    A. pay off forfeitures
    B. reward the bondsman who writes good bonds
    C. serve as a retirement nest egg
    D. reinvest in expanding the business

4. In checking the deed on a signer's property, it is important to remember that in most jurisdictions, land deeds are recorded

    A. alphabetically B. chronologically
    C. by scaled property value D. by address

5. In accepting real property as collateral on a bond, the
    I. property should be located nearby
    II. property should be completely paid for
    III. property should have increased in value since it was purchased
    IV. equity of the property should be equal to or greater than the bond amount
    The CORRECT answer is:

    A. I, II B. II, III, IV
    C. I, IV D. All of the above

6. The legal instrument that transfers ownership interest in real property to another party is a(n)

    A. warranty B. deed C. title D. easement

7. A defendant is in jail on $250,000 bond and the signers of the bail bond are offering real property as collateral. They paid $500,000 for the property 8 years ago, and they owe $300,000 on the property today.
    In order for the property to support the bond, it must be worth at LEAST _____ today.

    A. $400,000 B. $550,000 C. $630,000 D. $750,000

8. The judicial process by which the bonding company is relieved of all obligations and responsibilities associated with a posted bond is known as

    A. exoneration B. disposition
    C. acquittal D. dispensation

9. What is the legal term for defiance of a court's orders or authority?

   A. Ignominy
   B. Contumacy
   C. Contempt
   D. Recalcitrance

10. In order to write a face sheet, a bond agent uses the _____ provided by the jailer.

    A. power of attorney
    B. bail information sheet
    C. bail agreement
    D. application for bail

11. In order to expedite checking on the validity of a deed for property offered as collateral, an agent might attempt a business arrangement with

    A. the county recorder
    B. the county clerk
    C. a title insurance company
    D. the assessor's office

12. A signer to a deed has no substantial property assets to offer for collateral on a bond. If the agent wants to write the bond anyway, it is customary to require about _____ the cash value of the bond up front, plus the premium, as collateral.

    A. 10%   B. 33%   C. 50%   D. 100%

13. A _____ bond guarantees an answer to the obligee for the non-performance of the principal.

    A. surety
    B. performance
    C. fidelity
    D. court

14. As a general rule, an agent may accept real property as collateral on a bond if the bailor has been investing in the property for at LEAST _____ year(s).

    A. 1   B. 3   C. 5   D. 10

15. Which of the following is/are guidelines for an agent to follow in dealing with signers of bail agreements?
    I. Always try to get at least 2 signatures.
    II. Verify that a signer has been employed for at least 5 years.
    III. On bail that is set high, be willing to overlook a defendant's lack of employment if the signer has a solid employment history.
    IV. Require valid identification from all signers.

    The CORRECT answer is:

    A. I, IV   B. II, III   C. IV only   D. I, II

16. What type of real estate deed expresses a guarantee that the grantor holds official title and may legally sell the piece of property?

    A. Quitclaim deed
    B. Warranty deed
    C. Deed in trust
    D. Grant deed

17. If real property is offered as collateral on a bond, deeds should be examined most closely in cases in which the

    A. estate is a fee in tail
    B. defendant is being held on felony charges

C. last conveyance of the property took place more than 20 years ago
D. defendant has been arrested on forgery charges

18. After checking the deed of a property offered as collateral, an agent's next task would be to

    A. negotiate a premium with the signer
    B. determine the total value of the property
    C. write the bond agreement
    D. determine the amount of equity in the property

19. Typically, a bounty hunter's fee for a straight pickup amounts to _____ % of the total amount of the bond.

    A. 10   B. 15   C. 20   D. 40

20. A(n) _____ does NOT constitute an encumbrance on a property deed.

    A. lien
    B. mortgage
    C. restrictive covenant
    D. inadequate property description

21. The steps in the criminal justice process that occur following arrest and before an actual trial are often referred to as the _____ process.

    A. preliminary   B. arraignment
    C. hearing   D. accusatory

22. A defendant is in jail on $500,000 bond and the signer of the bail bond is offering real property as collateral. She paid $1,000,000 for the property 7 years ago, and she owes $600,000 on the property today. The property is now worth $1,400,000.
    What is the signer's equity in the property?

    A. $400,000   B. $600,000   C. $800,000   D. $1,100,000

23. An actual *bond* consists of the
    I. face sheet
    II. power of attorney
    III. application for bail
    IV. bail agreement
    The CORRECT answer is:

    A. I, II   B. II, III   C. III, IV   D. I, IV

24. In accepting a piece of real property as collateral on a bond, an agent becomes the holder of a(n) _____ deed.

    A. trust   B. grant   C. warranty   D. associate

25. Which of the following is a legal term for skipping town or otherwise avoiding court action through hiding or concealment?

    A. Decampment   B. Skip
    C. Jump   D. Abscond

KEY (CORRECT ANSWERS)

1. C
2. D
3. A
4. B
5. C

6. B
7. B
8. A
9. B
10. B

11. C
12. C
13. A
14. C
15. A

16. B
17. D
18. D
19. A
20. D

21. D
22. C
23. A
24. A
25. D

EXAMINATION SECTION
TEST 1

DIRECTIONS: Each question or incomplete statement is followed by several suggested answers or completions. Select the one that BEST answers the question or completes the statement. *PRINT THE LETTER OF THE CORRECT ANSWER IN THE SPACE AT THE RIGHT.*

1. New agents quickly learn that a policy fee is
    A. a one-time charge paid by a policy owner
    B. payable annually as part of the premium for a policy
    C. a policy tax assessed by states
    D. not payable on all policies offered by an insurer

2. In New York, a company licensed to do business there, but which has its home office in another state, would be classified as what type of company?
    A. Alien   B. Domestic   C. Native   D. Foreign

3. Converting a stock company into a mutual company is called a process of
    A. mutualization   B. transmutation   C. transformation   D. organization

4. If the policy owners have a right to vote for new directors of an insurance company, it is apparent that this is a _____ company.
    A. mono-line   B. mutual   C. casualty   D. stock

5. Identify an act of rebating.
    A. Persuading a policy owner to lapse an existing policy in order to buy a new policy
    B. Telling an applicant that a policy has no exclusions when it does
    C. Mailing birthday cards to clients
    D. Paying all expenses for a new policy owner's two-week trip to Canada

6. If an agent commingled premium money with his or her personal funds, he or she GENERALLY would be guilty of
    A. twisting   B. misrepresentation
    C. misusing premium funds   D. poor organization

7. What is the term that describes companies organized in a country other than the United States or its possessions?
    A. Foreign   B. Remote   C. Alien   D. Outside

8. Speaking disparagingly of a competitor's policy is unlawful and a form of
    A. misrepresentation   B. twisting
    C. fleecing   D. rebating

9. Regarding solicitors, the following statements are correct EXCEPT
    A. solicitors generally must be licensed
    B. the duties of agents and solicitors are identical
    C. a solicitor acts under the express authority of a licensed insurance agent
    D. the primary duty of solicitors is to locate prospects

10. All of the following would be rebating violations on the part of an agent EXCEPT

    A. paying Florida vacation expenses for a new policy owner
    B. sharing the commission with an applicant who purchases a policy
    C. buying a color television set for a policy owner
    D. taking a client to dinner

11. Underwriting techniques commonly used by insurers in issuing policies to applicants who do not measure up to a standard rating include the following EXCEPT

    A. attaching an exclusion rider or waiver to a policy
    B. averaging total risks pending
    C. charging an extra premium
    D. limiting the type of policy

12. Ethical business practices by an agent include which of the following?

    A. Advising a prospect that a competitor is new in the business.
    B. Placing the prospect's interest above the company interest.
    C. Recommending policies that meet the prospect's objectives.
    D. Agreeing with prospects when they have objections.

13. Which type of policy generally would require the MOST comprehensive underwriting?

    A. Accident
    B. Noncancellable and Guaranteed Renewable Disability Income
    C. Limited Risk
    D. Hospital Indemnity

14. All of the following are substandard rating systems EXCEPT

    A. make-up system
    B. lien system
    C. temporary flat extra premium
    D. extra percentage tables

15. In a health insurance transaction involving a broker, whom does the broker represent?

    A. Self
    B. The client
    C. The insurance company
    D. His or her agency

16. Twisting may involve any of the following actions on the part of an agent EXCEPT

    A. misrepresenting a proposed policy to a prospect
    B. making an incomplete comparison of policies
    C. misrepresenting a policy owner's existing policy
    D. converting a client's convertible term policy to permanent insurance

17. All of the following would constitute unlawful acts of rebating EXCEPT

    A. sharing a sales commission with a policy owner
    B. sending a new policy owner on an expense-paid trip to Florida
    C. sending birthday cards to a policy owner's children
    D. delivering a color television set to a policy owner as a Christmas gift

18. All of the following are examples of misrepresentation EXCEPT

    A. using a policy name that does not denote the true nature of the policy
    B. failing to explain truthfully a policy's terms or benefits
    C. unintentionally telling an applicant that a straight whole life policy will be paid up at 65
    D. pointing out a prospect that dividends are not guaranteed

19. All of the following statements concerning rebating are correct EXCEPT

    A. in some states, both the agent and the recipient are subject to penalties for a rebating violation
    B. rebating is not a form of discrimination
    C. an agent who is convicted of rebating may lose his or her license
    D. rebating occurs if an agent gives a buyer anything of significant value as an inducement to purchase a policy

20. According to the optional misstatement of age provision, the following statements are true EXCEPT if

    A. the insured actually was younger at the time of application than shown in the policy, benefits would be increased
    B. the insured really was older at the time of application than shown in the policy, benefits would be reduced
    C. the insured actually was older at the time of application than shown in the policy, the excess premiums paid would be refunded
    D. age of the insured is misstated at the time of application, all amounts payable under the policy would be what the premiums paid would have purchased at the correct age

21. Deductible provisions with major medical policies may be classified by any of the following terms EXCEPT

    A. integrated   B. flat   C. corridor   D. decreasing

22. All of the following are required policy provisions EXCEPT

    A. proofs of loss   B. entire contract and changes
    C. change of beneficiary   D. misstatement of age

23. All of the following specify owners' rights in a health insurance policy EXCEPT

    A. unpaid premium provision   B. incontestable provision
    C. grace period   D. reinstatement provision

24. Concerning the consideration for a health insurance policy, all of the following statements are correct EXCEPT

    A. the consideration clause may specify the insured's right to renew the policy
    B. two principal elements of the consideration are the premium payment and the application
    C. the amount and frequency of premium payment are stated in the consideration clause
    D. a consideration clause may be included in a rider if requested by the insured

25. Concerning the *free look* provision, all of the following statements are true EXCEPT
    A. most states require a free look provision in health insurance policies
    B. it permits policy owners to return their policies within a specified time and receive full refunds
    C. the company's risk is limited to the actual number of days the policy owner keeps the policy before returning it
    D. the policy owner need not give any reason for returning a policy in accordance with the provision

KEY (CORRECT ANSWERS)

1. B	11. B
2. D	12. C
3. A	13. B
4. B	14. A
5. D	15. B
6. C	16. D
7. C	17. C
8. A	18. D
9. B	19. B
10. D	20. C

21. D
22. D
23. A
24. D
25. C

TEST 2

DIRECTIONS: Each question or incomplete statement is followed by several suggested answers or completions. Select the one that BEST answers the question or completes the statement. *PRINT THE LETTER OF THE CORRECT ANSWER IN THE SPACE AT THE RIGHT.*

1. The word _____ relates DIRECTLY to the consideration clause. 1._____

    A. endorsement B. premium
    C. exclusion D. beneficiary

2. Under the required claim forms provision, it is the company's responsibility to supply claim forms to an insured within _____ days after receiving proof of loss. 2._____

    A. 21 B. 30 C. 7 D. 15

3. An application if filed for reinstatement of a policy, but the company takes NO action on such reinstatement. 3._____
   The policy is automatically reinstated after _____ days.

    A. 30 B. 45 C. 14 D. 20

4. In explaining franchise insurance, an agent may say that 4._____

    A. such plans may be either contributory or noncontributory
    B. it is sometimes called rental insurance
    C. small groups of persons can be covered in a master policy
    D. there is a savings in underwriting expense because a group of persons is insured in a single policy

5. The optional provision, other insurance in this insurer, is SPECIFICALLY designed to 5._____

    A. limit the risk with any one individual insured by the company
    B. avoid issuing two policies on an insured person
    C. restrict an insured's coverage to one type of accident and health insurance
    D. discount the premiums if more than policy is issued to insure the same individual

6. Under the optional provision, illegal occupation, which of the following applies if a loss occurs while the insured is participating in a felony or an illegal occupation? 6._____

    A. The insured's policy is automatically cancelled.
    B. The insurer is not liable for the loss.
    C. Benefits are reduced 50%.
    D. The insurer has a right to increase the premiums.

7. What is the document that defines the authority of an agent? 7._____

    A. Contract of Agency B. Rules of Authority
    C. Agent's Agreement D. Code of Ethics

8. A solicitor acts under the express authority of a(n) 8._____

    A. company B. agency C. client D. agent

13

9. Concerning agent licensing, which of the following statements is TRUE?

    A. Agent licenses are to be renewed annually.
    B. A person may be licensed without a company appointment.
    C. There are no temporary licenses.
    D. In some states, a specified number of approved pre-licensing study hours are required.

10. Giving a prospect or policy owner anything of significant value as an inducement to buy insurance is prohibited by law and is called

    A. discounting
    B. misrepresentation
    C. rebating
    D. twisting

11. Twisting pertains to the illegal act of an agent who

    A. induces a prospect to purchase more insurance than is needed to meet objectives
    B. persuades a prospect to lapse an existing policy in order to purchase a new policy
    C. shows the prospect one policy but has the prospect sign an application for a different policy
    D. persuades a prospect to buy more insurance than he or she can afford

12. A broker's contract is required for an agent who

    A. sells policies to corporations
    B. places policies with insurance companies other than the one with which he or she is under contract
    C. places a policy with a broker
    D. makes joint sales with another agent

13. From a technical standpoint, whom does the agent represent?

    A. Self
    B. Prospect
    C. Insurance company
    D. His or her agency

14. Any of the following would indicate moral hazard with a prospect EXCEPT

    A. poor credit rating
    B. excessive drinking
    C. use of drugs
    D. unmarried status

15. With an optionally renewable policy, the company reserves the right to

    A. cancel the policy anytime
    B. increase the premium on a policy if benefits paid to an insured exceed a stated amount
    C. modify the coverage if claims filed by the insured are excessive
    D. terminate coverage at any policy anniversary date or premium due date

16. All of the following relate DIRECTLY to owners' rights EXCEPT _____ provisions.

    A. reinstatement
    B. exclusions
    C. free look
    D. incontestable

17. Exclusions for pre-existing conditions help to avoid

    A. claims for long hospital confinements
    B. more complicated underwriting procedures

C. adverse selection against a company
D. insuring persons who are accident prone

18. There are _____ required uniform policy provisions.

    A. 9   B. 23   C. 12   D. 11

19. Under the required proofs of loss provision, a claimant normally is to submit proof of loss within 90 days; however, the *maximum* time limit is one year and that does NOT apply if the claimant

    A. did *not* find it reasonably possible to file proof of loss within one year
    B. did *not* have the legal capacity to comply
    C. moved from one state to another after loss occurred
    D. had recurring loss within six months

20. All of the following are sound reasons for agents to conduct policy delivery interviews with their clients EXCEPT

    A. helps to build a solid relationship with clients
    B. should be part of continuing service to clients
    C. provides a welcome break from routine paperwork in the office
    D. solidifies the sale

21. An applicant's signature *generally* is required on the following forms EXCEPT

    A. agent's report
    B. fair credit disclosure notice
    C. authorization to request medical information
    D. application

22. From a legal standpoint, constructive delivery of a policy is accomplished when the

    A. company sends the policy to the agent with instructions to obtain a statement attesting to the insured's good health
    B. agent delivers a policy for inspection but the initial premium has not yet been paid
    C. company relinquishes all control over the policy and turns it over to someone acting for the policy owner, including the company's own agent
    D. agent mails a policy to the policy owner with a note that he or she will stop by later to collect the first premium

23. There is a TOTAL of _____ uniform policy provisions.

    A. 23   B. 15   C. 11   D. 18

24. Suppose you interviewed Mildred M., an applicant, on October 1, 2007, and her date of birth is January 10, 1983.
    If the premium was to be based on her NEAREST birthday, what age would you have listed for her?

    A. 24   B. 23   C. 26   D. 25

25. How should the agent double check an applicant's age?
    A. Ask to see a driver's license.
    B. Measure the given age against the date of birth when filling in the application.
    C. Ask the applicant's spouse or close relative to confirm the age.
    D. Check the given age against a copy of the birth certificate.

KEY (CORRECT ANSWERS)

1. B
2. D
3. B
4. A
5. A

6. B
7. A
8. D
9. D
10. C

11. B
12. B
13. C
14. D
15. D

16. B
17. C
18. C
19. B
20. C

21. A
22. C
23. A
24. D
25. B

EXAMINATION SECTION
TEST 1

DIRECTIONS: Each question or incomplete statement is followed by several suggested answers or completions. Select the one that BEST answers the question or completes the statement. *PRINT THE LETTER OF THE CORRECT ANSWER IN THE SPACE AT THE RIGHT.*

1. Assume that a person, without any right to do so nor any reasonable ground to believe that he has such right, damages property of another person.
   According to the Penal Law, such a person would be guilty of all of the following EXCEPT criminal mischief in the _____ degree, if he _____.

    A. second; intentionally causes two thousand dollars' worth of damage
    B. fourth; intentionally damages property
    C. first; intentionally causes minor damage by means of an explosive
    D. fourth; recklessly damages property
    E. third; intentionally causes three hundred dollars' worth of damage

2. The Penal Law provides that in any prosecution for murder, it is an affirmative defense that the defendant acted under the influence of extreme emotional disturbance for which there was a reasonable explanation or excuse.
   According to the statute, the reasonableness of this explanation or excuse is to be determined from the viewpoint of

    A. the court
    B. a person in the defendant's situation
    C. the jury
    D. an ordinary prudent man
    E. a witness to the event

3. Following are four offenses of which possession of a deadly weapon other than a firearm MIGHT be an element:
    I. Burglary in the second degree
    II. Robbery in the first degree
    III. Robbery in the second degree
    IV. Criminal Trespass in the first degree

   According to the Penal Law, which of the following choices lists ALL of the above offenses of which possession of such deadly weapon IS an element?

    A. I, II
    B. II, III
    C. I, II, III
    D. I, II, IV
    E. I, II, III, IV

4. Intending to rob Smith of a watch, Jones knocks Smith to the ground without causing physical injury, and demands the watch from him. Upon learning that Smith does not have the watch in his possession, Jones runs away.
   According to the Penal Law, which of the following BEST explains whether or not Jones is guilty of attempted robbery in the third degree?
   Jones is

17

A. *not guilty* of an attempt since it was factually impossible for him to commit the robbery itself
B. *guilty* because he might have caused physical injury in the course of attempting the robbery
C. *not guilty;* since Smith did not have the watch in his possession, Jones has an affirmative defense
D. *guilty* since he could have committed the robbery if the surrounding circumstances were what he thought them to be
E. *not guilty* because there is no evidence that Smith resisted Jones' demand for the watch

5. Which of the following statements concerning assault is INCORRECT according to the Penal Law?
A person who

A. recklessly causes serious physical injury to another person is guilty of assault in the second degree
B. causes physical injury to another person by means of a deadly weapon may sometimes be guilty only of assault in the third degree
C. causes serious physical injury to another person without intent to cause such injury may sometimes be guilty of assault in the first degree
D. causes physical injury to an innocent person while in immediate flight from a robbery is guilty of assault in the second degree
E. causes another person to become unconscious, but does not cause physical injury, may sometimes be guilty of assault in the second degree

6. Following are three statements concerning the Homicide Section of the Penal Law that MIGHT be correct:
   I. A person who causes the death of another person, without any intent to cause death, may sometimes be guilty of murder
   II. When a participant in a robbery causes the death of an innocent person, another participant in the robbery may sometimes avoid liability for murder
   III. A person who intentionally aids another person to commit suicide may sometimes be guilty of murder

Which of the following choices lists ALL of the above statements that are CORRECT?

A. I only   B. I, III   C. II only
D. II, III   E. I, II, III

7. Each of the following statements describes property which has been obtained by means of larceny:
   I. A wallet containing $150 taken from a sleeping vagrant
   II. A credit card taken from a desk drawer
   III. Twenty rifles worth $100 each stolen from a sporting goods store
   IV. A bracelet worth $200 obtained by instilling in the victim a fear that a relative of hers will be injured.

According to the Penal Law, which of the following choices lists ALL of the above statements describing larceny for which grand larceny in the third degree would be the MOST serious offense?

A. I, II   B. I, IV
C. II, III   D. II, III, IV
E. I, II, III, IV

8. According to the Penal Law, as the result of a recent change in the corroboration requirements in sex offense cases, a person may not be convicted of sex offenses involving coercion solely on the testimony of the alleged victim unless there is other evidence which tends to

   A. establish every material fact essential to constitute the crime
   B. connect the defendant with the commission of the offense at the time of the alleged occurrence
   C. identify the defendant as the perpetrator
   D. establish that the alleged sexual conduct was actually consummated

8.____

9. Each of the following statements refers to the use of force by a person other than a peace officer when that person reasonably believes such to be necessary to prevent the commission of an offense.
According to the Penal Law, which of these statements is INCORRECT?
The person may use

   A. deadly physical force to prevent arson, even if he is not an owner of the threatened premises or privileged to be thereon
   B. deadly physical force to prevent burglary of a dwelling, if he is privileged to be in such dwelling
   C. physical force in order to prevent a crime involving damage to premises
   D. deadly physical force to prevent arson, if he is in control of the threatened premises
   E. physical force to prevent criminal trespass, even if he is not an owner of the threatened premises or privileged to be thereon

9.____

10. As a general rule, a witness in any legal proceeding, whether civil or criminal, may refuse to answer questions which will tend to show him guilty of a crime, or expose him to a penalty or forfeiture.
Relative to the right against self-incrimination, which of the following statements are TRUE?

   I. When one jurisdiction compels a witness to testify, after granting him immunity, such testimony may not be used to convict him of a crime in another jurisdiction.
   II. The privilege not only extends to answers that would expose the witness to self-incrimination but may be invoked to protect blood relatives.
   III. The protection afforded to a witness by the Fifth Amendment applies to lawyers as well as laymen.
   IV. It is solely within the determination of the witness to determine if by answering a question he would tend to incriminate himself.
   V. If a witness has already been tried for the crime in question or if the statute of limitations has run, he may be compelled to testify.

The CORRECT answer is:

   A. I, III, V   B. II, III, V   C. II, III, IV
   D. I, IV, V   E. I, II, IV

10.____

11. Prior to the interrogation of a person who is in police custody, certain warnings pursuant to the Miranda decision must be given to the detained individual.
Which of the following statements concerning these warnings is CORRECT?

   A. The best way to give the warnings is in writing and have the person in police custody read them and sign them.

11.____

B. It is sufficient merely to give the warnings to the person in police custody and then commence the questioning.
C. The person in police custody must knowingly, voluntarily, and intelligently acknowledge that he understands the warnings before he may be questioned.
D. The warnings should be given in the presence of the person's friends or relatives, or at least one of them, to provide evidence that the warnings were in fact given.
E. A statement made by a person in police custody who has not received the necessary warnings is never admissible at his trial.

12. Bill Walters, who has been subpoenaed as a witness to a holdup murder, is approached by two men, who offer him $1,000 to testify falsely as to what he had seen. When he refuses, they threaten his life. He then agrees, but notifies the police as soon as the two men leave.
According to the Penal Law, the two men can be charged with

A. subornation of perjury
B. perjury
C. suppressing evidence
D. dissuading witness from testifying

13. Arthur Mason has been released on $5,000 bail as the alleged armed robber of a supermarket. He fails to appear in court as ordered.
According to the Penal Law, it would be MOST correct for the police to charge Mason, in addition to the original charge, with a

A. felony for jumping bail, if he fails to surrender himself within 30 days
B. misdemeanor for jumping bail, if he fails to surrender himself within 30 days
C. felony for jumping bail, if he fails to surrender himself within 15 days
D. misdemeanor for jumping bail, plus the loss of the $5,000 if he fails to surrender himself within 15 days

14. Charging his pretty wife with infidelity, Joe Doakes has slashed at her face with a razor, causing severe mutilation around her eyes, mouth, and cheeks. This action results in permanent ugly scars. He is taken into custody and held for trial on a charge of maiming. In order to sustain this charge, it is necessary that intent be shown. According to the Penal Law, in connection with intent with respect to this crime, it is MOST correct to state that the

A. disfigurement need not even have been inflicted with felonious intent
B. injury must seriously diminish the victim's physical vigor
C. disfigurement must be incapable of being repaired by plastic surgery
D. mere infliction of the injury is presumptive evidence of the intent

15. John Smith, an accountant for the Chisler Corporation, is dismissed after 20 years with the organization. Angry and disgruntled with the treatment accorded to him by the company, Smith tells Bill Jones, a neighbor, about all he had done to build up the company. He tells Jones how *cheap* the company is and how easy it would be to rob it on any pay day because of the lack of protective devices. He says he hopes someone will do it some day, and goes into great detail about how it could be done successfully. About six months later, without any knowledge on Smith's part, Jones and his brothers, Jim and Bob, successfully rob the Chisler Corporation treasurer as he is about to pay off the staff. The holdup nets $40,000. Four years later, Bob Jones is appre

hended. He involves his brothers. Bill Jones, on questioning, describes how Smith had given him the idea for the crime.
According to the Penal Law, it would be MOST correct to state that Smith

- A. cannot be charged with having any connection with the crime because it took place entirely without his knowledge
- B. can no longer be arrested or charged with any crime because the statute of limitations for robbery is four years
- C. can be arrested and charged only with being an accessory because he took no part in the actual commission of the crime
- D. can be arrested and charged with being a principal to the robbery

16. John Doe, the defendant on a robbery charge, has been released on bail in Manhattan. He goes to the farm home of his parents in Ulster County and fails to appear in court as ordered. As a result, his bail is forfeited and a bench warrant is issued in New York County for his arrest.
The Criminal Procedure Law provides, with respect to the service of such a bench warrant, that it may

- A. not be served outside New York County, the county of issue
- B. be served in Ulster County, but only after being endorsed by a magistrate of that county
- C. be served in Ulster County without being endorsed by a magistrate of that county
- D. be served in any county, in the same manner as a warrant of arrest, without any exception

17. John Doe, a barber, who has been posing as a surgeon specializing in abortions, is on trial. He is charged with having performed an illegal abortion which resulted in the death of Jane X. Before she died, Jane X made a dying declaration naming Doe as the person who had performed the illegal operation.
According to the Criminal Procedure Law, it would be CORRECT to state that in this prosecution of Doe for abortion, Jane X's dying declaration shall

- A. be admitted in evidence without any restrictions
- B. be admitted in evidence subject to the same restrictions as in cases of homicide
- C. not be admitted in evidence
- D. not be admitted in evidence if Jane X voluntarily submitted to the operation fully aware of its possible consequences

18. The one of the following prerequisites for a permit to possess or dispose of firearms anywhere in this state, according to the Penal Law, is that the applicant MUST

- A. file a separate new application for each weapon if he wishes at any time to amend his license to include one or more weapons, if he is licensed either to possess weapons as an individual or as a dealer
- B. be a resident of the county in which the weapon is to be used if he is applying for a license to possess and carry a weapon as a merchant or employee of a financial institution
- C. not have been convicted of either a misdemeanor or a felony if he is applying for a permit to possess and carry concealable firearms
- D. be a citizen of the United States and over 21 years of age, if he wishes to be either a gunsmith or a dealer in firearms

19. Billy Doe, a 13-year-old boy, is the only witness to a crime committed by his 22-year-old uncle with whom he has been staying while on a visit to New York City.
According to the provisions of the Criminal Procedure Law, with respect to the production of the child in court, it would be CORRECT to state that a

   A. personal recognizance in writing shall be accepted from Billy's parent or guardian only
   B. separate personal recognizance must be taken by the court for each production of the child pending the final termination of the proceedings
   C. personal recognizance shall not be accepted in this case from any person
   D. personal recognizance shall be vacated on failure to produce Billy in court as ordered and Billy himself taken into custody thereafter

20. The hours during which a police officer of superior rank in the city must take bail for a misdemeanor are limited by the Criminal Procedure Law to the hours between

   A. 11 A.M. and 8 A.M. the next morning
   B. 2 P.M. and 8 A.M. the next morning
   C. 11 A.M. and 2 P.M. the same day
   D. 2 P.M. and 11 A.M. the next morning

21. John Doe has been arrested on a charge of disorderly conduct under the Penal Law. The one of the following offenses covered by this law for which the Criminal Procedure Law requires the court's approval prior to admitting him to bail is

   A. jostling against or unnecessarily crowding a person in a public place
   B. acting in such a manner as to interfere with others
   C. congregating on a public street and refusing to move on when ordered by the police
   D. shouting outside a building at night to the annoyance of a considerable number of persons

22. John Doe has been arrested by an officer on patrol at night and brought to the station house for booking on a charge of disorderly conduct under the Penal Law.
According to the Criminal Procedure Law, the desk officer MUST release Doe on bail for appearance before a magistrate the next morning if Doe was charged with

   A. interfering with a person by placing his hand near such person's pocketbook or pocket
   B. soliciting men for lewd purposes in a public place
   C. engaging in an illegal occupation
   D. causing a disturbance in a bus or acting in a manner disturbing or offensive to others

23. John Doe has been arrested in New York County charged therein with murder, first degree.
According to the Criminal Procedure Law, it would be CORRECT to state, with respect to the release of Doe on bail, that he

   A. can be released on bail by a justice of the Supreme Court of New York State
   B. can be released on bail by a justice of the Court of Special Sessions of the City of New York

C. cannot be released on bail by anyone if he had ever before attempted to commit a felony
D. cannot be released on bail under any circumstances, except by a judge of the district court

24. Peter Poe has been arrested on a charge of petit larceny. A search of police files indicates prior convictions for possessing a dangerous weapon and for illegally using the same.
According to the Criminal Procedure Law, it would be CORRECT to state, with respect to the release of Poe on bail when arraigned in the court indicated, that he

   A. can be released on bail by a judge of the district court because such judges can admit to bail perpetrators of any crime
   B. can be released on bail by a judge of the criminal court of the city because petit larceny is a misdemeanor
   C. cannot be released on bail by a judge of the criminal court of the city because Poe has had two prior convictions
   D. cannot be released on bail by a judge of the district court, because such judges can only admit to bail defendants charged with an offense

25. According to the Penal Law, with regard to the use of force or fear in the crime of robbery, it would be MOST correct to state that, to constitute robbery,

   A. force may have been used to obtain possession of the property, but, if this did not occur, force must have been used to escape
   B. the mere snatching of the property from the hand of the victim without his resistance and without force or violence by the offender is sufficient
   C. fear is a necessary ingredient regardless of the value of the property taken
   D. when there is nothing to inspire fear, superior force must have been used, and the property relinquished upon a struggle and upon compulsion

KEY (CORRECT ANSWERS)

1. D
2. B
3. D
4. D
5. A

6. E
7. A
8. C
9. E
10. A

11. C
12. C
13. A
14. D
15. A

16. C
17. B
18. D
19. C
20. B

21. A
22. D
23. A
24. B
25. D

TEST 2

DIRECTIONS: Each question or incomplete statement is followed by several suggested answers or completions. Select the one that BEST answers the question or completes the statement. *PRINT THE LETTER OF THE CORRECT ANSWER IN THE SPACE AT THE RIGHT.*

1. All the means by which any alleged matter of fact, the truth of which is submitted to investigation, is established or disproved, is the legal definition of

    A. proof
    B. burden of proof
    C. evidence
    D. admissibility of evidence

2. That section of an affidavit in which an officer empowered to administer an oath certifies that this document was *sworn to* before him is called a(n)

    A. affirmation
    B. jurat
    C. acknowledgement
    D. verification

3. In legal terminology, a *bailee* is a person who

    A. lawfully holds property belonging to another
    B. deposits cash or property for the release of an arrested person
    C. has been released from arrest on a bond that guarantees his court appearance
    D. deposits personal property as collateral for a debt

4. A specimen of handwriting of known authorship which can be used by an investigator for making a comparison with a questioned or suspected writing is called a(n)

    A. inscription
    B. precis
    C. coordinate
    D. exemplar

5. According to the Criminal Procedure Law, the decision of the judge presiding in the court in which the crime is triable is final with respect to bail. An order denying bail is non-appealable and so any attack on such a denial of bail must be by other means.
The *other means* is by resort to the prisoner's separate and different right to test the legality of his detention by a

    A. writ of coram nobis
    B. writ of habeas corpus
    C. writ of certiorari
    D. certificate of reasonable doubt

6. The one of the following statements with respect to bail which is CORRECT is that

    A. a person who has a previous conviction for a felony can be admitted to bail
    B. a desk officer is required to take bail in bailable cases between the hours of 11 A.M. of one day and 9 A.M. the next morning
    C. if an application for admission to bail is denied by a judge, no application can be made to other judges
    D. the *offenses* mentioned in the Criminal Procedure Law are not bailable by a desk officer or a judge

7. The Police Department has generally supported legislation amending the Criminal Procedure Law (relating generally to bail) which would authorize the fingerprinting and photographing of gamblers on arrest in order to

   A. reduce the number of veteran bookmakers actively engaged in bookmaking
   B. permit the imposition of high bail which would eliminate the practice of bail jumping
   C. enable the court to have the prior criminal record of the defendant when bail is fixed
   D. validate and supplement the Known Gamblers File

8. X, intending to rob Y, points an unloaded revolver at him. The element which makes the assault involved here *assault, second degree* is the fact that

   A. there is no intent to kill
   B. the revolver is unloaded
   C. the injury, if any were sustained, would be relatively light
   D. the intent is thus shown to be to secure property and not to inflict grave bodily harm

9. With respect to policy and bookmaking, it can be stated that the one of the following which is NOT true of both is that

   A. the player is equally guilty
   B. each can be called a *continuous offense*
   C. if an auto is used, it should be seized as evidence
   D. the *lookout* is liable to arrest

10. One of the defenses available to one accused of crime is that of entrapment. The defense of entrapment is LEAST likely to be met with in _____ cases.

    A. narcotics
    B. prostitution
    C. gambling
    D. rape

11. According to the Penal Law, a person who operates or drives any vehicle of any kind in a reckless or culpably negligent manner, whereby a human being is killed, should be charged MOST properly with

    A. criminal negligence in the operation of a vehicle resulting in death
    B. manslaughter in the second degree
    C. manslaughter in the first degree
    D. vehicular homicide

12. Failure by an operator or chauffeur to exhibit his license to a peace officer shall be _____ evidence that he is not duly licensed.

    A. conclusive
    B. corroborative
    C. circumstantial
    D. presumptive

13. With respect to the review of convictions in state courts by the Supreme Court of the United States, the latter has stated that, so far as due process affects admissions before trial of the defendant, the accepted test of the admissibility of such admissions is their

    A. voluntariness
    B. timeliness
    C. materiality
    D. motivation

3 (#2)

14. A very important rule in the law of evidence is that known as the *best evidence rule*. This rule applies to

    A. documents
    B. judicial notice
    C. eyewitness testimony
    D. oral testimony

15. The one of the following statements which is LEAST correct, according to the Criminal Procedure Law, is that a peace officer may arrest a person

    A. without a warrant for a felony when he has reasonable cause for believing that a felony has been committed and that the person arrested committed it
    B. with a warrant at any hour of the day or night for any crime provided the arrest is made in the same county where the warrant was issued
    C. without a warrant when a felony has in fact been committed and he has reasonable cause for believing the person to be arrested to have committed it
    D. at night with a warrant for a misdemeanor when directed by the issuing judge's endorsement upon the warrant

16. The one of the following statements concerning arrests by private persons which is INCORRECT is:

    A. A private person who has arrested another for the commission of a crime must deliver him to a peace officer
    B. A private person may arrest another for a crime committed or attempted in his presence
    C. A private person makes an arrest for a felony at his peril if he arrests the wrong person
    D. Except when making an arrest during the actual commission of a crime or on pursuit immediately after its commission, a private person before making an arrest must inform the person to be arrested of the cause thereof, and require him to submit

17. A recent change in the Criminal Procedure Law, in relation to filing complaints against a youthful offender so that he nay be adjudged a wayward minor, provides that a new class of individuals who may lay such information before the judge is that of

    A. peace officers
    B. other persons standing in parental relation as being the next of kin
    C. principals or teachers of any school where such person is registered for attendance
    D. representatives of an incorporated society doing charitable or philanthropic work

18. It has been suggested that in reducing a confession to writing it is desirable to include several errors and to have the person making the confession make the corrections and sign or initial them.
    The one of the following which MOST supports this suggestion is that such corrections by the person making the confession

    A. helps to minimize the credibility of possible later denials concerning the material set forth in the confession
    B. is likely to encourage the investigator to continue his investigation on the corrected matter and thereby discourages a complete reliance on the confession itself

C. provides additional and new evidence which links the person making the confession to the crime charged
D. provides additional corroboration of facts which only the person making the confession would know about

19. Fingerprints should be taken of any person arrested and charged with   19._____

    A. libel
    B. exposure of person in a public place
    C. soliciting alms on a public street
    D. adultery

20. A person who, while in the act of committing a felony, carnally abuses the body of a child sixteen years of age or under   20._____

    A. shall receive the additional sentence provided for under the Penal Law
    B. may be sentenced to an indeterminate term of one day to life imprisonment
    C. shall for the purpose of sentencing be deemed a second offender and punished accordingly
    D. shall be sentenced to life imprisonment

21. Which of the following statements is CORRECT?   21._____

    A. The permissible number of peremptory jury challenges is divided by the number of defendants.
    B. In a case with 4 defendants, one of them need not join in an effective peremptory challenge of jurors.
    C. The permissible number of peremptory jury challenges for the defense is multiplied by the number of defendants.
    D. In a case with multiple defendants, all defendants must join for a peremptory challenge of jurors to be effective.

22. The replacement of a juror by an alternate juror   22._____

    A. may be done at will before trial
    B. may require defendant's consent in certain circumstances
    C. never requires defendant's consent
    D. always requires defendant's consent

23. When a jury visits premises involved in a case,   23._____

    A. if one party is present, the other side must also be present, and vice versa
    B. defendant's right to be present may be waived
    C. all parties, and the court, must be present
    D. the defendant must be present

24. A trial order of dismissal   24._____

    A. may be granted at any stage of a trial
    B. disposes of a criminal action in the same manner as acquittal by verdict
    C. may be appealed by the People on the ground that evidence offered was erroneously excluded
    D. may not be appealed

25. Requests to charge a jury
    A. may be made orally only by the People, after the court's charge
    B. may be made orally only by defendant, after the court's charge
    C. must be made in writing before the charge, but may be oral thereafter
        be made orally or in writing, by either side, before or after the court's charge

---

KEY (CORRECT ANSWERS)

1. C
2. B
3. A
4. D
5. B

6. A
7. C
8. B
9. A
10. D

11. A
12. D
13. A
14. A
15. B

16. A
17. C
18. A
19. B
20. B

21. B
22. B
23. B
24. C
25. D

TEST 3

DIRECTIONS: Each question or incomplete statement is followed by several suggested answers or completions. Select the one that BEST answers the question or completes the statement. *PRINT THE LETTER OF THE CORRECT ANSWER IN THE SPACE AT THE RIGHT.*

1. A child under the age of sixteen may be convicted of the crime of

   A. felony murder
   B. murder, 2nd degree
   C. manslaughter, 1st degree
   D. manslaughter, 2nd degree

   1.____

2. There are NO degrees of the crime of

   A. sodomy   B. perjury   C. forgery   D. fraud

   2.____

3. In cases of prostitution, complaints against offenders are drawn under the Criminal Procedure Law because

   A. fines imposed for violations of this statute are payable into the city treasury rather than the state treasury
   B. a heavier penalty is imposed for violations of that law than is imposed for violation of pertinent sections of the Penal Law
   C. under this law the testimony of the arresting officer as a matter of law does not require corroboration
   D. violations of pertinent sections of the Penal Law are offenses only rather than crimes

   3.____

4. Under the Penal Law, a person who perpetrates an act of sexual intercourse with an unmarried female, not his wife, with her consent is guilty of a misdemeanor only if

   A. the girl is over eighteen years of age
   B. he is under the age of eighteen
   C. previous chaste character of the girl is not shown
   D. there is no corroboration of the female's testimony

   4.____

5. The assault of a person by administering poison to him

   A. is assault in the first degree in all cases
   B. is assault in the second degree in all cases
   C. is assault in the third degree in all cases
   D. may be assault in the first or second degree depending on the circumstances

   5.____

6. Because of the nature of the underlying crime, a person could not be convicted of felony murder committed while engaged in the commission of

   A. treason   B. arson
   C. kidnapping   D. malicious mischief

   6.____

7. A child over seven and under sixteen years of age who, without just cause and without the consent of his parents, deserts his home is defined in the Penal Law as a

   A. delinquent child
   B. neglected child
   C. wayward child
   D. youthful offender

8. A person could be convicted of an attempt to commit burglary who

   A. planned a burglary and started in an automobile to commit it but was arrested before he reached the building he intended to break and enter
   B. attempted to break and enter a building but who became frightened and ran away before effecting either a break or entry
   C. approached a house with the intent of breaking and entering it but who, upon reaching it, changed his mind and burned it instead
   D. not knowing the purpose for which they would be used, furnished another with the tools employed in breaking and entering burglarized premises

9. A person who wilfully in any manner encourages or assists another person in taking his life is guilty of

   A. murder in the second degree
   B. manslaughter in the first degree
   C. manslaughter in the second degree
   D. suicide

10. In order to establish the crime of kidnapping, it is NOT necessary to show

    A. that actual force was used
    B. the existence of a specific criminal intent
    C. that the taking was against the will of the victim
    D. that there was no lawful authority for the taking

11. A conviction for seduction does NOT require proof

    A. of sexual intercourse
    B. of previous chaste character of the female
    C. that the female was under eighteen
    D. of a promise of marriage or fraudulent representation of marriage

12. A person who made oral threats in order to obtain property of another can be convicted of the felony of extortion only if it is shown that the

    A. threats were to injure the person or property of the person threatened by another
    B. victim actually parted with property
    C. victim parted with his property against his will
    D. threats were made under color of official right

13. The corroboration required in the case of the testimony of an accomplice

    A. must be sufficient to establish the corpus delicti
    B. must refer to all the material elements of the crime charged
    C. need only show that the crime has been committed
    D. need only connect the defendant with the commission of the crime

14. A public officer who, unlawfully and maliciously under color of official authority, does an act whereby another person is injured in his person, property or rights, commits the crime of   14.____

    A. embracery   B. champetry
    C. coercion   D. oppression

15. The crime of arson in the first degree can be committed   15.____

    A. in the daytime
    B. by burning an unoccupied dwelling house
    C. by burning a building other than a dwelling house
    D. by burning an uninhabited building in the night time

16. A, a resident of X County, reported the theft of his automobile in Y County. The automobile was subsequently found in the possession of B in Z County.   16.____
    An indictment for the larceny of the automobile may be found in

    A. X, Y, or Z County   B. Y or Z County
    C. Y County *only*   D. Z County *only*

17. A statutory exception whereby a police officer may make an arrest for a misdemeanor though not committed in his presence is   17.____

    A. smoking in the subway
    B. keeping a disorderly house
    C. jostling
    D. peddling without a license
    E. leaving scene of an accident

18. A, finding the door of the B Warehouse unlocked, pushed it open and went inside the warehouse. When apprehended by Patrolman C, he was examining the contents of the safe which he had apparently opened.   18.____
    Of the following, the MOST appropriate charge against A is that of

    A. burglary   B. trespass
    C. petty larceny   D. malicious mischief
    E. robbery

19. A robbed B of his diamond ring valued at $250 and hid it in C's home with C's knowledge and consent. C *double-crossed* A and offered to sell the ring to D for one-half its value, telling D that it had been stolen by A. D purchased the ring.   19.
    On the basis of these facts,

    A. C is guilty of a felony and D of a misdemeanor
    B. D is guilty of no crime
    C. C is guilty of both a felony and misdemeanor
    D. C and D are both guilty of a felony
    E. C and D are both guilty of a misdemeanor

20. A takes $50 at 1:00 A.M. from B's pocket while B is asleep on the porch of his home.   20.____
    Of the following, the crime that has been committed is MOST accurately described as

    A. grand larceny, 1st degree
    B. grand larceny, 2nd degree

C. petty larceny
D. robbery, 1st degree
E. robbery, 2nd degree

21. Jones and Smith were partners in a business venture. According to their agreement, each was allowed to draw checks on the funds of the partnership. Jones drew a check to himself for $200 against the funds of the partnership and cashed the check, using the $200 for his personal pleasure.
Of the following, the statement which is MOST correct concerning this situation as stated is that

   A. Jones is guilty of embezzlement of funds of the partnership
   B. Jones could not be held on a charge of embezzlement
   C. only a charge of robbery could be placed against Jones
   D. Jones could be prosecuted for obtaining money under false pretenses
   E. premeditated grand larceny could be charged against Jones

22. M, in great pain and believing himself to be dying, said, *My brother N did not murder O. I murdered O.* M died the next day. At the trial of N for the murder of O, the statement of M was not admitted as a dying declaration.
This was so PRIMARILY because

   A. the great pain of M probably affected his mental processes and judgment
   B. M's statement did not concern his own death
   C. M did not die shortly after the confession
   D. M was a relative of N
   E. it could be proved that shortly before he died, M thought he was recovering

23. As soon as practicable after an arrest, the arresting officer should inform the arrested person of the offense or conduct for which the arrest is made.
Of the following, the MOST appropriate reason for this procedure is that

   A. such procedure will usually prevent resistance on the part of the person being arrested
   B. the person being arrested will have his fear of assault or robbery allayed
   C. a good public relations policy dictates the need for full communication between officer and the arrested person
   D. immediate disclosure of the reason for arrest will reduce possible complaints of improper police conduct
   E. it affords the arrested person an opportunity to determine his legal rights or defense, or both

Questions 24-25.

DIRECTIONS: Questions 24 and 25 are to be answered on the basis of the following paragraph.

A person who, with the intent to deprive or defraud another of the use and benefit of property or to appropriate the same to the use of the taker, or of any other person other than the true owner, wrongfully takes, obtains or withholds, by any means whatever, from the possession of the true owner or of any other person any money, personal property, thing in action, evidence of debt or contract, or article of value of any kind, steals such property and is guilty of larceny.

24. This definition from the Penal Law has NO application to the act of   24._____

   A. fraudulent conversion by a vendor of city sales tax money collected from purchasers
   B. refusing to give proper change after a purchaser has paid for an article in cash
   C. receiving property stolen from the rightful owner
   D. embezzling money from the rightful owner
   E. stealing property which the rightful owner intends to give away

25. According to the foregoing paragraph, an auto mechanic who claimed to have a lien on   25._____
an automobile for completed repairs and refused to surrender possession until the bill was paid

   A. *cannot* be charged with larceny, because his repairs increased the value of the car
   B. *can* be charged with larceny, because such actual possession can be construed to include intent to deprive the owner of use of the car
   C. *cannot* be charged with larceny, because the withholding is temporary and such possession is not an evidence of debt
   D. *can* be charged with larceny, because he is wrongfully withholding the car from the true owner by questionable means
   E. *cannot* be charged with larceny, because intent to defraud is lacking

KEY (CORRECT ANSWERS)

1. B		11. C	
2. D		12. B	
3. C		13. D	
4. B		14. D	
5. D		15. C	
6. A		16. B	
7. A		17. E	
8. B		18. A	
9. B		19. D	
10. A		20. A	

21. B
22. B
23. E
24. C
25. E

EXAMINATION SECTION
TEST 1

DIRECTIONS: Each question or incomplete statement is followed by several suggested answers or completions. Select the one that BEST answers the question or completes the statement. *PRINT THE LETTER OF THE CORRECT ANSWER IN THE SPACE AT THE RIGHT.*

Questions 1-12.

DIRECTIONS: Questions 1 through 12 are based on the Criminal Procedure Law. Each question consists of two statements. Mark your answer.
- A. if only sentence I is correct
- B. if only sentence II is correct
- C. if sentences I and II are correct
- D. if neither sentence I nor II is correct

1. I. Except as otherwise provided in the Criminal Procedure Law, a prosecution for a misdemeanor must be commenced within three years after the commission thereof.
    II. Except as otherwise provided in the Criminal Procedure Law, a prosecution for a petty offense must be commenced within two years after the commission thereof. 1.____

2. I. A person may not be prosecuted twice for the same offense. 2.____
    II. A defendant may not be convicted of any offense upon the testimony of an accomplice unsupported by corroborative evidence tending to connect the defendant with the commission of such offense.

3. I. A defendant may testify in his own behalf, but his failure to do so is not a factor from which any inference unfavorable to him may be drawn. 3.____
    II. A child less than twelve years old may not testify under oath in a criminal proceeding in a court of law.

4. I. A person may be convicted of an offense solely upon evidence of a valid confession or admission made by him without additional proof that the offense charged has been committed. 4.____
    II. Evidence of a written or oral confession, admission, or other statement made by a defendant with respect to his participation or lack of participation in the offense charged may not be received in evidence against him in a criminal proceeding if such statement was involuntarily made.

5. I. A summons may be served by a police officer, or by a complainant at least eighteen years of age, or by any other person at least eighteen years old designated by the court. 5.____
    II. A summons may be served anywhere in the county of issuance or anywhere in an adjoining county in the state.

6. I. Any person may arrest another person for a felony anywhere in the state when the latter has in fact committed such felony. 6.____
    II. Any person may arrest another person for any offense other than a felony when the latter has in fact committed such offense in his presence, provided that the arrest is made only in the county in which such offense was committed.

35

7. I. A search warrant must be executed not more than three days after the date and time of issuance and it must thereafter be returned to the court without unnecessary delay.
    II. No search warrant may be executed unless the police officer gives notice of his authority and purpose to the occupant of the premises or vehicle to be searched. In addition, the police officer must serve a copy of the warrant upon the occupant of said premises or vehicle.

7.____

8. I. An appearance ticket may be issued by a police officer following an arrest without a warrant if the arrest was for a Class B misdemeanor but not if the arrest was for a Class A misdemeanor.
    II. An appearance ticket may, at the discretion of the police officer or other public servant authorized to issue appearance tickets, be served either personally or by registered or certified mail, return receipt requested.

8.____

9. I. Under the *Youthful Offender Treatment* article of the Criminal Procedure Law (Article 720), *youth* means a person charged with a crime who was at least sixteen years old and less than nineteen years old at the time of his alleged commission of such crime.
    II. When an individual has been adjudged eligible for youthful offender treatment, he may be found guilty by reason of a preponderance of the evidence rather than guilty based upon proof beyond a reasonable doubt.

9.____

10. I. A police officer may arrest a person without a warrant for any offense, other than for a petty offense, when he has reasonable cause to believe that such person has committed such offense, whether in his presence or otherwise.
    II. A police officer may arrest a person for a petty offense without a warrant when such offense was committed in the officer's presence, within the geographical area of such police officer's employment, and such arrest is made in the county where such offense was committed.

10.____

11. I. A police officer may stop a person in a public place located within the geographical area of such officer's employment when he reasonably suspects that such person is committing, has committed or is about to commit either (a) a felony or (b) any misdemeanor as defined in the penal law, and may demand of him his name, address, occupation, the name and address of his employer, and an explanation of his conduct.
    II. Whenever a police officer stops a person in a public place for temporary questioning, he may search such person for a deadly weapon or any instrument, article or substance readily capable of causing serious physical injury and of a sort not ordinarily carried in public places by law-abiding persons.

11.____

12. I. A defendant in any criminal action who is less than eighteen years old may refuse to permit himself to be fingerprinted unless accompanied by a parent or legal guardian.
    II. A police officer who is executing an arrest warrant need not have the warrant in his possession; if he has not, he must show it to the defendant upon request as soon after the arrest as possible.

12.____

Questions 13-24.

DIRECTIONS: Questions 13 through 24 are to be answered SOLELY on the basis of the Penal Law.

13. A person is guilty of grand larceny in the first degree when he steals property which

   A. consists of personal property valued at more than $1500
   B. is obtained by instilling in the victim a fear that that the victim's membership in a subversive organization will be revealed
   C. consists of goods valued in excess of $250
   D. is obtained by instilling in the victim a fear that an antique vase which he owns will be damaged

14. Using or threatening the immediate use of a dangerous instrument is an element of all of the following offenses EXCEPT _____ in the _____ degree.

   A. robbery; first
   B. burglary; first
   C. robbery; second
   D. burglary; second

15. Which of the following describes a person guilty of escape in the first degree?

   A. A person convicted of a felony escapes from a detention facility.
   B. A person just convicted of a misdemeanor escapes from a courtroom by impersonating a police officer.
   C. A person escapes from a police officer's custody by causing serious physical injury to the officer.
   D. After committing a felony, a person escapes from the scene of the crime by using or threatening the immediate use of a deadly weapon.

16. A person who wantonly and recklessly fires a rifle into a crowd of people without any specific intent to injure or kill would NOT be guilty of

   A. murder if death results
   B. assault in the first degree if serious physical injury results
   C. assault in the second degree if physical injury results
   D. reckless endangerment in the first degree if no injury results

17. Each of the following choices states an offense involving the forcible stealing of property, and certain additional facts.
    In which choice would the defendant be guilty of the offense stated, based SOLELY on the facts given in the choice? Robbery in the

   A. first degree - defendant robs a bank while carrying two sticks of dynamite, which cannot be seen under his jacket
   B. second degree - while defendant and his partner are fleeing from a store they have just robbed, the partner pushes a bystander to the ground, thereby causing a painful bruise to bystander's shoulder
   C. first degree - while robbing a bank, defendant threatens to kidnap and kill the manager's wife unless the manager gives him all the money in the vault
   D. second degree - defendant robs a jewelry store, while his partner waits in a getaway car parked around the corner

18. A person is ALWAYS guilty of a felony if he unlawfully possesses   18.____

    A. any loaded firearm in a vehicle
    B. any deadly weapon and is not a citizen of the United States
    C. any dagger or razor with intent to use the same unlawfully against another
    D. a shotgun in a building used for educational purposes

19. Knowing that Jones intends to rob a bank, Smith gives Jones a rifle to use during the   19.____
    robbery. However, the day before the robbery is supposed to occur, the police arrest
    Jones on an old charge, thereby preventing the robbery.
    Based on these facts, it would be CORRECT to state that Smith is

    A. *not guilty* of any crime
    B. *guilty* of conspiracy in the second degree and criminal facilitation in the second degree
    C. *guilty* of criminal facilitation in the second degree but is not guilty of conspiracy in the second degree
    D. *guilty* of conspiracy in the second degree but is not guilty of criminal facilitation in the second degree

20. Each of the following choices states an offense involving the death of a person, and certain additional facts.   20.____
    In which choice would the defendant NOT be guilty of the offense stated, based SOLELY on the facts given in the choice?

    A. Manslaughter in the second degree - when the defendant intentionally causes or aids another person to commit suicide
    B. Murder - when the defendant and two other persons attempt to commit escape in the second degree, and one of the participants causes the death of a person other than one of the participants
    C. Manslaughter in the first degree - when with intent to cause serious physical injury to another person, the defendant causes the death of a third person
    D. Murder - when the defendant engages in conduct which creates a grave risk of death of another person, and thereby causes the death of another person

21. Which of the following elements would raise the crime of custodial interference from the second degree to the first degree?   21.____

    A. The intent to hold a child permanently or for a protracted period
    B. Exposure of the person taken to a risk that his health will be materially impaired
    C. The taking of a child less than sixteen years old from his lawful custodian
    D. Enticement of an incompetent person from lawful custody

22. Which one of the following elements must ALWAYS be present for a person to be guilty of arson in the first degree?   22.____

    A. The presence in the building at the time of another person who is not a participant in the crime
    B. Intentional damage to a building caused by a fire
    C. Knowledge by the person that another person not a participant in the crime is present in the building
    D. Circumstances which render the presence in the building of another person not a participant in the crime a reasonable possibility

23. For which of the following crimes is it a necessary element that a person knowingly enter or remain unlawfully in a dwelling, as the word *dwelling* is defined in the Penal Law?

 23.____

   A. Criminal trespass in the first and second degree
   B. Criminal trespass in the second degree and burglary in the first degree
   C. Criminal trespass in the first degree and burglary in the second degree
   D. Burglary in the first and second degree

24. Assume that the police stop a car in which three men are riding. Ward is the driver, and Jones and King are passengers. During a lawful search, the police find one-quarter ounce of morphine concealed in King's coat. Based SOLELY on these facts, it would be CORRECT to state that

 24.____

   A. King, Jones, and Ward are all guilty of criminal possession of a dangerous drug
   B. a presumption of knowingly possessing the morphine applies to Ward but not to Jones
   C. King is guilty of criminal possession of a dangerous drug and Ward is guilty of conspiracy
   D. King is guilty of criminal possession of a dangerous drug but Ward and Jones are not

---

KEY (CORRECT ANSWERS)

1.	D	11.	D
2.	A	12.	B
3.	C	13.	D
4.	B	14.	C
5.	C	15.	A
6.	C	16.	C
7.	D	17.	B
8.	D	18.	A
9.	A	19.	A
10.	C	20.	D

21. B
22. A
23. B
24. D

# TEST 2

DIRECTIONS: Each question or incomplete statement is followed by several suggested answers or completions. Select the one that BEST answers the question or completes the statement. *PRINT THE LETTER OF THE CORRECT ANSWER IN THE SPACE AT THE RIGHT.*

1. Which of the following statements is(are) CORRECT?
   The Criminal Procedure Law (CPL) applies to
   I. all criminal actions and proceedings commenced on or after September 1, 1971, and appeals and other post-judgment proceedings relating thereto.
   II. criminal actions and proceedings commenced before September 1, 1971 but pending thereafter
   III. appeals and other post-judgment proceedings commenced on or after September 1, 1971 which relate to criminal actions and proceedings commenced or concluded prior thereto, provided that, where application of CPL would not be feasible or would work injustice, the former Code of Criminal Procedure shall apply
   IV. criminal procedure matters occurring on or after September 1, 1971 which are not a part of any particular action or case
   The CORRECT answer is:

   A. All of the above
   B. I *only*
   C. I, II, III
   D. II, III, IV

2. Which of the following is hearsay?
   A(n)

   A. written statement by a person not present at the court hearing where the statement is submitted as proof of an occurrence
   B. oral statement in court by a witness of what he saw
   C. written statement of what he saw by a witness present in court
   D. re-enactment by a witness in court of what he saw

3. In a criminal case, a statement by a person not present in court is

   A. *acceptable* evidence if not objected to by the prosecutor
   B. *acceptable* evidence if not objected to by the defense lawyer
   C. *not acceptable* evidence except in certain well-settled circumstances
   D. *not acceptable* evidence under any circumstances

4. The rule on hearsay is founded on the belief that

   A. proving someone said an act occurred is not proof that the act did occur
   B. a person who has knowledge about a case should be willing to appear in court
   C. persons not present in court are likely to be unreliable witnesses
   D. permitting persons to testify without appearing in court will lead to a disrespect for law

5. One reason for the general rule that a witness in a criminal case MUST give his testimony in court is that

   A. a witness may be influenced by threats to make untrue statements
   B. the opposite side is then permitted to question him
   C. the court provides protection for a witness against unfair questioning
   D. the adversary system is designed to prevent a miscarriage of justice.

6. An appeal MAY be taken from a

   A. verdict
   B. judgment
   C. decision
   D. conviction

7. Jury trial commences

   A. with the selection of a jury
   B. when the defendant makes opening address
   C. when the first opening address is made
   D. when the first witness is sworn

8. Adjective criminal law is governed PRIMARILY by the

   A. Penal Law
   B. Civil Practice Law and Rules
   C. Criminal Procedure Law
   D. Code of Criminal Procedure

9. Which of the following contain(s) references included in the definition of *warrant of arrest?*
   - I. Process of local criminal court to produce defendant for arraignment
   - II. Produce defendant for arraignment upon filed accusatory instrument
   - III. Addressed to peace officer to produce defendant for arraignment
   - IV. Process of any criminal court requiring defendant to appear before it for arraignment on a prosecutor's information

   The CORRECT answer is:

   A. I, II, III, IV
   B. III *only*
   C. I, II, III
   D. I, II, IV

10. Superior courts have jurisdiction in the following areas:
    - I. Unlimited trial jurisdiction of all offenses
    - II. Exclusive trial jurisdiction of felonies
    - III. Concurrent trial jurisdiction of misdemeanors
    - IV. Preliminary jurisdiction of all offenses, exercised only through grand juries

    The CORRECT answer is:

    A. I *only*
    B. I, II
    C. I, II, III
    D. II, III, IV

11. Petty offense means

    A. all violations and traffic infractions
    B. some misdemeanors and all violations
    C. only conduct which is not a traffic infraction and is punishable by imprisonment for not more than 15 days
    D. a class B misdemeanor only

12. An offense committed near a boundary between two adjoining counties of this state may be prosecuted in either of such counties.
    The MAXIMUM distance from a county border is

    A. 1,000 feet   B. 1,000 yards   C. 500 feet   D. 500 yards

13. A felony is committed on the Hudson River south of the northern boundary of New York City.
    The county or counties having jurisdiction to try the case is(are)

    A. New York, Richmond, Bronx, Kings, and Queens Counties
    B. New York, Richmond, and Bronx Counties
    C. New York and Richmond Counties only
    D. New York County only

14. A crime is committed on a bus regularly carrying passengers from Nassau County to Manhattan by way of Queens. At the time of the occurrence, the bus is in Nassau on its way to its terminal point – Manhattan. The victim is a Queens resident. The alleged perpetrator is a resident of Manhattan.
    The county or counties having jurisdiction in this case is(are)

    A. Nassau or New York   B. Nassau or Queens
    C. Nassau, Queens, or Manhattan   D. Nassau only

15. Prosecution of a crime MUST be commenced within

    A. one year after commission, for all misdemeanors and petty offenses
    B. two years after commission, for all misdemeanors and petty offenses
    C. 5 years after commission, for all felonies
    D. 5 years after commission, for some felonies

16. A private person in making an arrest is limited as follows:

    A. For an offense, at any hour of day or night
    B. For a crime only, at any hour of any day or night
    C. For a felony only, at any hour of any day or night
    D. All of the above

17. An appearance ticket directs a specific person to appear in a criminal court in connection with the alleged commission of a designated offense.
    This appearance ticket may be issued only by a

    A. local criminal court judge
    B. local criminal court judge or police officer
    C. police officer or authorized public servant
    D. police officer, authorized public servant, or local criminal court judge

18. An arrest by a private person without a warrant can PROPERLY be made in which one of the following situations?

    A. There is reasonable cause to believe that the person being arrested committed a felony.
    B. The person arrested for a felony has in fact committed the felony.
    C. The person arrested for a misdemeanor has in fact committed the misdemeanor.
    D. The person arrested for any offense has in fact committed the offense.

19. A peace officer, outside the geographical area of his employment, has reasonable cause to believe that a felony was committed in his presence.
In the circumstances,

   A. he may make an arrest, without restriction
   B. he may make an arrest only on the same authority as that of a private person
   C. he may make an arrest during the commission of the felony, immediately thereafter or during immediate flight
   D. none of the above

19.____

20. After making an arrest, a police officer must perform all required recording, fingerprinting, and other related duties.
He MUST do so

   A. immediately
   B. without unnecessary delay
   C. within 24 hours
   D. within 8 hours

20.____

21. A police officer, acting without a warrant, may arrest a person

   A. only in the geographical area of his employment
   B. outside the geographical area of his employment only for a felony
   C. without restriction, for a petty offense committed anywhere in the state
   D. for a crime committed anywhere in the state

21.____

22. Summons is a process whose SOLE function is to

   A. commence a criminal action
   B. substitute for a warrant of arrest, where a warrant may not be issued
   C. produce defendant for arraignment upon a filed accusatory instrument
   D. inform defendant as to nature of the offenses charged

22.____

23. A summons may be served by

   A. any person without restriction
   B. any person at least 18 years old
   C. a police officer, without restriction
   D. a peace officer, without restriction

23.____

24. An arrest warrant is addressed to and can be executed by

   A. any adult person
   B. a police officer or classification of police officers
   C. a peace officer or classification of peace officers
   D. any person over the age of 18, not a party to the action

24.____

25. Which of the following would invalidate an acknowledgment?

   A. Failure to say deponent is known to notary
   B. Seal is missing
   C. Acts done on Sunday
   D. Affiant misspells his name

25.____

KEY (CORRECT ANSWERS)

1.	A	11.	A
2.	A	12.	D
3.	C	13.	A
4.	A	14.	A
5.	B	15.	D
6.	B	16.	A
7.	A	17.	C
8.	C	18.	B
9.	D	19.	C
10.	D	20.	B

21. D
22. C
23. C
24. B
25. A

TEST 3

DIRECTIONS: Each question or incomplete statement is followed by several suggested answers or completions. Select the one that BEST answers the question or completes the statement. *PRINT THE LETTER OF THE CORRECT ANSWER IN THE SPACE AT THE RIGHT.*

1. A warrant of arrest may be executed anywhere in the state   1._____

    A. without restriction, if it is issued by a city court
    B. in all cases, without restriction
    C. in all cases, provided it is appropriately endorsed by a local criminal court of the county where the arrest is to be made
    D. when issued by the city criminal court

2. A warrant of arrest may be executed on any day   2._____

    A. of the week, at any hour
    B. except Sunday, at any hour of the day; but on Sunday only between 9:00 A.M. and 6:00 P.M.
    C. including Sunday, provided it is so endorsed by the issuing court
    D. except Sunday

3. A police officer or court officer of a criminal court may stop a person, under specified circumstances, when he reasonably suspects that the person is committing, has committed, or is about to commit any felony   3._____

    A. or a Class A misdemeanor defined in the Penal Law
    B. or misdemeanor defined in the Penal Law
    C. or any misdemeanor only
    D. only

4. At a hearing on a felony complaint, defendant   4._____

    A. may testify in his own behalf within the discretion of the court, but he has a right to call witnesses
    B. has a right to testify in his own behalf, but he may call witnesses only within the discretion of the court
    C. has a right to testify in his own behalf and to call witnesses
    D. may testify in his own behalf, within the discretion of the court, and call witnesses in his behalf, within the discretion of the court

5. A grand jury, to be legally constituted, MUST consist of _____ members.   5._____

    A. not less than 16 and not more than 23
    B. not less than 12 and not more than 16
    C. not less than 12 and not more than 23
    D. at least 12

6. At a preliminary hearing on a felony complaint,   6._____
    I. the defendant must be present
    II. the defendant has a right to be present, but he may waive this right
    III. the defendant has a right to call witnesses in his behalf
    IV. all witnesses called may be cross-examined

The CORRECT answer is:

A. I, II   B. II, III   C. I, IV   D. II, IV

7. The number and term of grand juries empanelled for a court are determined generally by

   A. Supreme Court in the county, on application of the District Attorney showing the estimated need
   B. Rules of the court for which the grand jury is drawn
   C. Judicial Conference regulations
   D. Appellate Division rules

8. The quantum of proof required for a court to hold a defendant for grand jury action on a felony complaint is proof

   A. affording the court reasonable cause to believe
   B. sufficient for a reasonable man
   C. by a fair preponderance of the evidence
   D. beyond a reasonable doubt

9. The acting foreman of a grand jury is

   A. chosen by lot
   B. chosen by the court
   C. the second grand juror to be empanelled
   D. chosen by the grand jurors

10. When a grand jury requires legal advice, they may receive it

    A. only from the court, District Attorney, or an attorney designated by either
    B. either from the court or District Attorney, only
    C. only from the District Attorney
    D. only from the court

11. In all cases, when a motion is made for a change of venue, a(n)

    A. application for a stay, denied by a Supreme Court justice, may not thereafter be granted by a justice of the Appellate Division
    B. application for a stay, denied by a Supreme Court justice, may be reviewed and granted by a justice of the Appellate Division
    C. stay may be granted only by any Supreme Court justice in the judicial district
    D. stay may be granted by any superior court judge in the judicial district

12. Evidence of mental disease or defect as a trial defense excluding criminal responsibility is admissible

    A. only as to a defendant who has previously been examined under court order by two qualified psychiatrists
    B. provided the defendant has served and filed timely written notice of intention to rely thereon
    C. provided the People have served a demand on the defendant to give notice of this defense
    D. in all cases without restriction

13. On a defense of alibi,
    A. the People in all cases are entitled on trial to an adjournment not in excess of 3 days
    B. a court may receive testimony as in D below but on application must grant an adjournment of not less than 7 days
    C. a court may not receive testimony as in D below
    D. a court may receive testimony, in its discretion, from a witness who was not included in defendant's notice of alibi

14. Which of the following statements are CORRECT?
    I. The People, having the burden of proof, address the jury before defendant at all stages.
    II. A closing address to the jury by the prosecution is required.
    III. A closing address to the jury by both sides is discretionary.
    IV. An opening address to the jury by both sides is discretionary.
    V. The People in all cases must make an opening address to the jury.
    The CORRECT answer is:
    A. I, II, III
    B. II, III, IV
    C. I, II, IV
    D. I, II, V

15. In selecting a jury, the MAXIMUM total number of challenges to alternate jurors that may be exercised by BOTH parties is
    A. 16
    B. 8
    C. 4
    D. 2

16. A grand jury witness may be called only on request of the
    A. court, District Attorney, or grand jury
    B. court
    C. District Attorney or the grand jury
    D. grand jury

17. A prospective defendant in a grand jury proceeding who wishes the grand jury to hear a witness in his behalf is limited by the fact that
    A. the grand jury, in its discretion, may hear the witness if the defendant makes an oral or written request
    B. the grand jury must hear the witness if the defendant makes an oral or written request
    C. the grand jury must hear the witness only if the defendant makes a written request
    D. there may be no legal basis for such a request

18. When a charge has been dismissed by a grand jury following its consideration of the matter, which of the following is CORRECT?
    A. It may be resubmitted to successive grand juries by court order, without limitation.
    B. It may be resubmitted to a grand jury if a court so authorizes, but no further submission thereafter is permissible.
    C. Without court order, it may be considered by another grand jury, but not by the same grand jury.
    D. It may again be considered by the same grand jury, without court order.

19. An indictment MUST contain
    I. endorsement, *A True Bill,* signed by the district attorney
    II. applicable section number of the statute allegedly violated
    III. date or period when alleged conduct occurred
    IV. statement in each court that the grand jury accuses the defendant of a designated offense

    The CORRECT answer is:

    A. I, II, IV
    B. III, IV
    C. II, III, IV
    D. I, II, III, IV

19.____

20. With respect to an offense raised to higher grade by reason solely of a previous conviction, which of the following statements is CORRECT?

    A. Under no circumstances is a jury permitted to know of the previous conviction.
    B. The order of trial is in this instance substantially the same as in other cases, except for arraignment on a special information.
    C. Before any proceeding to establish defendant's identity and previous conviction, he must be advised of the privilege against self-incrimination.
    D. The defendant's conviction of the predicate case may be established at any time before the case goes to the jury.

20.____

21. The term *petty offense* includes

    A. no misdemeanors, some violations, all traffic infractions
    B. no misdemeanors, but all violations and traffic infractions
    C. some misdemeanors, all violations and traffic infractions
    D. all misdemeanors, violations, and traffic infractions

21.____

22. Conviction, as defined in CPL, means

    A. entry of guilty plea, or guilty verdict
    B. serving of sentence
    C. entry of final judgment
    D. imposition and entry of sentence

22.____

23. With regard to a non-jury trial, which of the following is CORRECT?

    A. Trial commences when both parties appear, are ready, and the court announces that the case is on trial. The court's determination as to guilt or innocence is properly termed a verdict.
    B. If there is no opening address, trial commences when the first witness is sworn, and the court's determination as to guilt or innocence is properly termed a verdict.
    C. An opening address, if made, commences the trial, and the court's determination of guilt or innocence is properly termed a decision.
    D. There must be an opening address to the court; this commences the trial; and the court's determination of guilt or innocence is properly termed a decision.

23.____

24. In relation to double jeopardy, a person may not be twice prosecuted for the same offense.
    Assuming the same offense, which of the following does NOT relate to double jeopardy under CPL?

24.____

A. Defendant is found not guilty after trial in one jurisdiction
B. An accusatory instrument is filed in a court of another country
C. An accusatory instrument is filed in a Federal court
D. An accusatory instrument is filed in a state other than New York

25. Which of the following is NOT applicable to a warrant of arrest? 25.____

   A. Its function is to produce defendant for arraignment.
   B. It commences a criminal action.
   C. It is issued only by a local criminal court.
   D. It is addressed to a police officer.

KEY (CORRECT ANSWERS)

1.	D	11.	A
2.	A	12.	B
3.	A	13.	D
4.	B	14.	D
5.	A	15.	A
6.	D	16.	C
7.	D	17.	A
8.	A	18.	B
9.	B	19.	B
10.	B	20.	B

21. B
22. A
23. B
24. B
25. B

EXAMINATION SECTION
TEST 1

DIRECTIONS: Each question or incomplete statement is followed by several suggested answers or completions. Select the one that BEST answers the question or completes the statement. *PRINT THE LETTER OF THE CORRECT ANSWER IN THE SPACE AT THE RIGHT.*

1. R forcibly stole property from Z.
   Which one of the following additional elements, if present, would MOST properly justify charging R with robbery in the first degree, rather than robbery in the third degree?
   R

   A. punched Z during the robbery, giving Z a black eye
   B. used a motor vehicle to escape from the robbery scene
   C. was aided by an accomplice when committing the robbery
   D. produced a knife and threatened to use it, but did not stab Z, when committing the robbery
   E. produced a gun and threatened to use it during the robbery. The gun was unloaded but Z did not know this.

2. Patrolman P, having received information from a reliable third party that Z had committed a misdemeanor, arrests Z without a warrant and drives him to the lockup. As Z is being transferred from the patrol car to the lockup, he breaks away from P and runs into a crowd of persons. After a ten-minute foot chase, P reapprehends Z.
   Which one of the following BEST states the offense or offenses, if any, for which P may now properly arrest Z without a warrant?

   A. Only escape in the third degree
   B. Only escape in the second degree
   C. Only the misdemeanor for which he was originally arrested
   D. P may not properly arrest Z for any of the above offenses
   E. The misdemeanor for which he was originally arrested, and escape in the third degree

3. A stolen car with three occupants is stopped after a high speed chase and the occupants are arrested. P, one of the occupants, has an unloaded, but operable, .32 caliber pistol tucked in his belt, and six .32 caliber rounds in his pocket. U, the second occupant, has an unloaded, but operable, .45 caliber pistol in his pants' pocket and has no bullets on his person. L, the driver, has neither a pistol nor any ammunition on his person. When the vehicle is searched, a loaded .38 caliber pistol is found under the right front seat. None of the occupants of the car has ever been convicted of a crime and none has a valid license for any of the weapons.
   Which one of the following BEST states which weapon or weapons each man may properly be charged with felonious possession of?

   A. P, U, and L may each properly be charged with felonious possession of only the .32 and the .38.
   B. P, U, and L may each properly be charged with felonious possession of the .32, the .38, and the .45.

C. P may properly be charged only with felonious possession of the .32, and both U and L may not be properly charged with the felonious possession of any of the weapons.
D. P may properly be charged with felonious possession of only the .32, U may properly be charged only with the felonious possession of the .45, and L may not be properly charged with the felonious possession of any of the weapons.
E. P may properly be charged with felonious possession only of the .32 and the .38, U may properly be charged with felonious possession only of the .45 and the .38, and L may properly be charged with felonious possession only of the .38.

4. Following are three situations in which a police officer might possibly be justified in using deadly physical force upon another person:
   I. To prevent the escape of an unarmed person who was seen by the officer snatching a woman's purse
   II. To arrest an unarmed person observed by the officer committing arson
   III. To arrest an unarmed person when the officer reasonably believes that the person is likely to inflict serious physical injury to a third party unless apprehended without delay, under conditions that do not amount to imminent use of deadly physical force

Which one of the following choices lists ALL of the above cases in which a police officer is actually justified in using deadly physical force and NONE in which he is not?
He is

A. justified in I, II, and III
B. not justified in I, II, or III
C. justified in I and III, but not in II
D. justified in II but not in I and III
E. justified in II and III, but not in I

5. L lends R a pistol, believing that R intends to use the pistol to rob V. During the robbery, with which L had no further part, R kills V.
Which one of the following, if any, is the MOST serious crime with which L may properly be charged?

A. Conspiracy in the fourth degree
B. Criminal facilitation in the first degree
C. Criminal facilitation in the second degree
D. Criminal solicitation in the second degree
E. None of the above, since he may not properly be charged with any crime

6. Which one of the following is LEAST likely to be a degree-raising factor for the crime of assault?
That

A. a dangerous instrument was used
B. the assailant was over 18 years of age when the assault occurred
C. serious physical injury rather than ordinary physical injury was caused
D. physical injury was caused intentionally rather than recklessly
E. physical injury was inflicted in the course of the commission of an independent felony

7. R and S, while planning an armed robbery of an armored truck, study the route taken by the truck from a bank to a factory where payroll money is delivered every Thursday. A bartender hears their conversation and informs the police. Part of the plan involves staging an automobile accident along the route taken by the truck, and robbing the truck when the driver stops. On the day of the intended robbery, the route taken by the truck is altered so that it will not pass by the location where R and S have staged the accident; and R and S, both heavily armed, are arrested by police at the scene.
Which one of the following is the MOST serious crime with which R and S may properly be charged?

   A. Robbery in the first degree
   B. Conspiracy in the third degree
   C. Conspiracy in the second degree
   D. Attempted robbery in the first degree
   E. Attempted robbery in the second degree

8. The section of the State Penal Law dealing with murder has been modified in several respects. One such modification concerned an aspect of the *felony murder* doctrine of the law.
Which one of the following is both the MOST accurate statement as to how the felony murder doctrine was modified and also the APPARENT legislative intent therefor?

   A. Listing certain specific felonies, to clarify the meaning of the term *any felony* in the former statute
   B. Including all felonies under the felony murder doctrine, so that a fatality which occurs during the commission of any felony is punishable as murder
   C. Including all felonies in which a motor vehicle is used, either in committing the felony or in escaping from the scene, so that fatalities which occur in these cases are punishable as murder
   D. Excluding certain non-violent felonies from the felony murder doctrine, so that a fatality which is either accidental or which the perpetrator cannot reasonably foresee is not punishable as murder
   E. Adding the necessity of proving intent as an element of murder in non-violent felonies, so that a fatality in connection with a non-violent felony is not punishable as murder when intent cannot be proved

9. While on duty, P, a police officer, received from his superior a description of Z, who was involved in a robbery, and believed to be in P's area. The superior officer's information concerning Z's involvement in the robbery came from a reliable third party. P observes a person closely matching Z's description. When P approaches, the person starts to run, but is quickly apprehended and placed under arrest for robbery. While searching this person for weapons, P discovers a quantity of narcotics in his inside coat pocket and forthwith seizes the narcotics.
Which one of the following MOST properly evaluates both whether or not the seizure of the narcotics was proper in this case and also the BEST reason therefor?
The seizure was

   A. *proper,* but only because narcotics are contraband
   B. *proper,* since it was made incident to a lawful arrest
   C. *improper,* since P did not have an arrest warrant for Z
   D. *improper,* since P did not have probable cause for arrest
   E. *improper,* since the narcotics were unrelated to the crime for which the arrest was made

10. Following are three situations in which *Miranda* warnings were not given when the confessions made by the persons involved might possibly be admissible as evidence:
A person
   I. walks into a police station and volunteers a statement to the desk sergeant implicating himself in a robbery
   II. in prison for committing a certain crime, being questioned concerning his involvement in a second crime, confesses to the second crime
   III. arrested at the scene of a robbery attempt, being questioned concerning the crime, confesses to the crime

Which one of the following choices lists all of the above situations in which the confession is ADMISSIBLE and none in which it is NOT?
The confession is admissible in

A. I, but not in II and III
B. I and II, but not in III
C. I, II, and III
D. I and III, but not in II
E. III, but not in I and II

KEY (CORRECT ANSWERS)

1.	D	6.	B
2.	D	7.	D
3.	A	8.	D
4.	D	9.	B
5.	C	10.	A

TEST 2

DIRECTIONS: Each question or incomplete statement is followed by several suggested answers or completions. Select the one that BEST answers the question or completes the statement. *PRINT THE LETTER OF THE CORRECT ANSWER IN THE SPACE AT THE RIGHT.*

1. According to the Criminal Procedure Law, the decision of the judge presiding in the court in which the crime is triable is final with respect to bail. An order denying bail is non-appealable and so any attack on such a denial of bail must be by other means.
   The *other means* is by resort to the prisoner's separate and different right to test the legality of his detention by a

   A. writ of coram nobis
   B. writ of habeas corpus
   C. writ of certiorari
   D. certificate of reasonable doubt

   1.____

2. X, intending to rob Y, points an unloaded revolver at him.
   The element which makes the assault involved here assault, second degree, is the fact that

   A. there is no intent to kill
   B. the revolver is unloaded
   C. the injury, if any were sustained, would be relatively light
   D. the intent is thus shown to be to secure property and not to inflict grave bodily harm

   2.____

3. One of the defenses available to one accused of crime is that of entrapment.
   The defense of entrapment is LEAST likely to be met with in _____ cases.

   A. narcotics   B. prostitution
   C. gambling   D. rape

   3.____

4. With respect to the review of convictions in state courts by the Supreme Court of the United States, the latter has stated that, so far as due process affects admissions before trial of the defendant, the accepted test of the admissibility of such admissions is their

   A. voluntariness   B. timeliness
   C. materiality   D. motivation

   4.____

5. A very important rule in the law of evidence is that known as the *best evidence rule*.
   This rule applies to

   A. documents   B. judicial notice
   C. eyewitness testimony D. oral testimony

   5.____

6. The one of the following statements which is LEAST correct, according to the Criminal Procedure Law, is that a peace officer may arrest a person

   A. without warrant for a felony when he has reasonable cause for believing that a felony has been committed and that the person arrested committed it
   B. with a warrant at any hour of the day or night for any crime provided the arrest is made in the same county where the warrant was issued

   6.____

C. without a warrant when a felony has in fact been committed and he has reasonable cause for believing the person to be arrested to have committed it
D. at night with a warrant for a misdemeanor when directed by the issuing judge's endorsement upon the warrant

7. The one of the following statements concerning arrests by private persons which is INCORRECT is:

   A. A private person who has arrested another for the commission of a crime must deliver him to a peace officer
   B. A private person may arrest another for a crime committed or attempted in his presence
   C. A private person makes an arrest for a felony at his peril if he arrests the wrong person
   D. Except when making an arrest during the actual commission of a crime or on pursuit immediately after its commission, a private person before making an arrest, must inform the person to be arrested of the cause thereof, and require him to submit

8. A change in the Criminal Procedures Law in relation to filing complaints against a youthful offender so that he may be adjudged a wayward minor provides that a new class of individuals who may lay such an information before the judge is that of

   A. peace officers
   B. other persons standing in parental relation as being the next of kin
   C. principals or teachers of any school where such person is registered for attendance
   D. representatives of an incorporated society doing charitable or philanthropic work

9. Persons apprehended by Federal agents in conjunction with city police in many narcotics arrests are frequently tried under the State law in a State court.
   Of the following, the PRINCIPAL reason for this procedure is that

   A. more expeditious handling of the case is assured due to the unusually heavy caseload in the Federal courts in the city
   B. it is then not necessary to reveal the identity of the Federal agents involved in an arrest
   C. the penalties in the state courts are more certain and usually more drastic
   D. state courts are less severe with respect to the admissibility of certain kinds of evidence

10. It has been suggested that in reducing a confession to writing it is desirable to include several errors and to have the person making the confession make the corrections and sign or initial them.
    The one of the following which MOST supports this suggestion is that such corrections by the person making the confession

    A. helps to minimize the credibility of possible later denials concerning the material set forth in the confession
    B. is likely to encourage the investigator to continue his investigation on the corrected matter and thereby discourages a complete reliance on the confession itself

C. provides additional and new evidence which links the person making the confession to the crime charged
D. provides additional corroboration of facts which only the person making the confession would know about

KEY (CORRECT ANSWERS)

1. B
2. B
3. D
4. A
5. A
6. B
7. A
8. C
9. D
10. A

EXAMINATION SECTION
TEST 1

DIRECTIONS: Each question or incomplete statement is followed by several suggested answers or completions. Select the one that BEST answers the question or completes the statement. *PRINT THE LETTER OF THE CORRECT ANSWER IN THE SPACE AT THE RIGHT.*

1. The delivery of an arrested person to his sureties, upon their giving security for his appearance at the time and place designated to submit to the jurisdiction and judgment of the court, is known as
   A. bail
   B. habeas corpus
   C. parole
   D. probation

   1._____

2. Jones was charged with the murder of Smith. Brown, Jones' landlord, testified at the trial that Jones had in his home a well-equipped laboratory which contained all the necessary chemical for producing the poison which an autopsy showed caused Smith's death.
   Brown's testimony constitutes what is called _____ evidence.
   A. corroborative   B. opinion   C. hearsay   D. circumstantial

   2._____

3. In addressing a class of recruits, a police lieutenant remarked: "Carelessness and failure are twins."
   The one of the following that MOST NEARLY expresses his meaning is
   A. negligence seldom accompanies success
   B. incomplete work is careless work
   C. conscientious work is never attended by failure
   D. a conscientious person never makes mistakes

   3._____

4. In taking a statement from a person who has been shot by an assailant and is not expected to live, police are instructed to ask the person: "Do you believe you are about to die?"
   Of the following, the MOST probable reason for this question is
   A. the theory that a person about to die will tell the truth
   B. to determine if the victim is conscious and capable of making a statement
   C. to put the victim mentally at ease and more willing to talk
   D. that the statement could not be used in court if his mind was distraught by the fear of impending death

   4._____

5. If, while you are on duty at a busy intersection, a pedestrian asks you for directions to a particular place, the BEST course of conduct is to
   A. ignore the question and continue directing operations
   B. tell the pedestrian to ask a patrolman on foot patrol
   C. answer the question in a brief, courteous manner
   D. leave your post only long enough to give clear and adequate directions

   5._____

6. In lecturing on the law of arrest, a lieutenant remarked: "To go beyond is as bad as to fall short."
   The one of the following which MOST NEARLY expresses his meaning is
   A. never undertake the impossible   B. extremes are not desirable
   C. look before you leap   D. too much success is dangerous

7. Suppose you are an officer assigned to a patrol precinct. While you are in the vicinity of a school, your attention is called to a man who is selling small packages to school children. You are told that this man distributes similar packages to these same children daily and that he is suspected of dealing in narcotics.
   Of the following, the BEST action for you to take is to
   A. pretend to be an addict and attempt to purchase narcotics from him
   B. observe the man's action yourself for several days in order to obtain grounds for arrest
   C. stop and question one or more of the children after they have transacted business with the man
   D. stop and question the man as he leaves the children

8. In the event of a poison gas attack, civil defense authorities advise civilians to _____ door and windows and go to _____.
   A. open; upper floors   B. close; upper floors
   C. open; the basement   D. close; the basement

9. The procedure whereby a defendant is brought before a magistrate, informed of the charge against him, and asked how he pleads thereto, is called
   A. arraignment   B. indictment   C. presentment   D. inquisition

10. A written accusation of a crime presented by a grand jury is called a(n)
    A. commitment   B. arraignment   C. indictment   D. demurrer

11. The one of the following statements made by a prisoner that is correctly called an alibi is:
    A. "He struck me first."
    B. "I didn't intend to hurt him."
    C. "I was miles away from there at the time."
    D. "I don't remember what happened."

12. A person who, after the commission of a crime, conceals the defender with the intent that the latter may escape from arrest and trial, is called a(n)
    A. accessory   B. accomplice   C. confederate   D. associate

13. A sworn statement of fact is called a(n)
    A. affidavit   B. oath
    C. acknowledgment   D. subpoena

14. The right of trial by jury in the courts of the state is PRIMARILY safeguarded by a provision of
    A. the United States Constitution
    B. the constitution of the state
    C. a state statute
    D. a Federal statute

15. The task of protecting the President and his family is entrusted PRIMARILY to the
    A. Federal Bureau of Investigation
    B. United States Secret Service
    C. Central Intelligence Agency
    D. District of Columbia Police Department

16. The coordinating organization for the various Federal agencies engaged in intelligence activities is the
    A. Federal Bureau of Investigation
    B. Federal Security Agency
    C. Mutual Security Agency
    D. Central Intelligence Agency

17. A drug addict whose arm shows many scars from the injection of a hypodermic needle is MOST apt to be addicted to
    A. heroin   B. cocaine   C. opium   D. marijuana

18. All of the following drugs are derived from opium EXCEPT
    A. cocaine   B. heroin   C. morphine   D. codeine

19. In addition to cases of submersion, artificial respiration is a recommended first aid procedure for
    A. sunstroke
    B. chemical poisoning
    C. electric shock
    D. apoplexy

20. An injury to a muscle or tendon brought about by severe exertion and resulting in pain and stiffness is called a
    A. strain   B. sprain   C. bruise   D. fracture

21. Of the following kinds of wounds, the one in which there is the LEAST danger of infection is a(n) _____ wound.
    A. abrasive   B. punctured   C. lacerated   D. incised

22. When a person is found injured on the street, it is generally advisable, pending arrival of a physician, to help prevent fainting or shock by keeping the patient
    A. in a sitting position
    B. lying down with the head level
    C. lying down with the head raised
    D. standing on his feet

23. When an injured person appears to be suffering from shock, of the following, it is MOST essential to
    A. loosen his clothing
    B. keep him warm
    C. administer a stimulant
    D. place him in a prone position

24. In the sentence, "Malice was immanent in all his remarks," the word "immanent" means MOST NEARLY
    A. elevated   B. inherent   C. threatening   D. foreign

25. In the sentence, "The extant copies of the document were found in the safe," the word "extant" means MOST NEARLY
    A. existing   B. original   C. forged   D. duplicate

26. In the sentence, "The recruit was more complaisant after the captain spoke to him," the word "complaisant" means MOST NEARLY
    A. calm   B. affable   C. irritable   D. confident

27. In the sentence, "The man was captured under highly creditable circumstances," the word "creditable" means MOST NEARLY
    A. doubtful   B. believable   C. praiseworthy   D. unexpected

28. In the sentence, "His superior officers were more sagacious than he," the word "sagacious" means MOST NEARLY
    A. shrewd   B. obtuse   C. absurd   D. verbose

29. In the sentence, "He spoke with impunity," the word "impunity" means MOST NEARLY
    A. rashness   B. caution   C. without fear   D. immunity

30. In the sentence, "The new patrolman displayed unusual temerity during the emergency," the word "temerity" means MOST NEARLY
    A. fear   B. rashness   C. calmness   D. anxiety

31. In the sentence, "The portions of food were parsimoniously served," the word "parsimoniously means MOST NEARLY
    A. stingily   B. piously   C. elaborately   D. generously

32. In the sentence, "Generally the speaker's remarks were sententious," the word "sententious means MOST NEARLY
    A. verbose
    C. argumentative
    B. witty
    D. pithy

33. In the sentence, "The prisoner was fractious when brought to the station house," the word "fractious" means MOST NEARLY
    A. penitent   B. talkative   C. irascible   D. broken-hearted

34. In the sentence, "The judge was implacable when the attorney pleaded for leniency," the word "implacable" means MOST NEARLY
    A. inexorable
    C. inattentive
    B. disinterested
    D. indifferent

35. In the sentence, "The court ordered the mendacious statements stricken from the record," the word "mendacious" means MOST NEARLY
    A. begging   B. lying   C. threatening   D. lengthy

36. In the sentence, "The district attorney spoke in a strident voice," the word "strident" means MOST NEARLY
    A. loud
    B. harsh-sounding
    C. sing-song
    D. low

37. In the sentence, "The speaker had a predilection for long sentences," the word "predilection" means MOST NEARLY
    A. aversion
    B. talent
    C. propensity
    D. diffidence

38. In the sentence, "The candidate wants to file his application for preference before it is too late," the word "before" is used as a(n)
    A. preposition
    B. subordinating conjunction
    C. pronoun
    D. adverb

39. The one of the following sentences which is grammatically PREFERABLE to the others is:
    A. Our engineers will go over your blueprints so that you may have no problems in construction.
    B. For a long time he had been arguing that we, not he, are to blame for the confusion.
    C. I worked on this automobile for two hours and still cannot find out what is wrong with it.
    D. Accustomed to all kinds of hardships, fatigue seldom bothers veteran policemen.

40. The plural of
    A. turkey is turkies
    B. cargo is cargoes
    C. bankruptcy is bankruptcys
    D. son-in-law is son-in-laws

41. The abbreviation "viz." means MOST NEARLY
    A. namely
    B. for example
    C. the following
    D. see

42. In the sentence, "A man in a light-grey suit waited thirty-five minutes in the ante-room for the all-important document," the word IMPROPERLY hyphenated is
    A. light-grey
    B. thirty-five
    C. ante-room
    D. all-important

43. The MOST accurate of the following sentences is:
    A. The commissioner, as well as his deputy and various bureau heads, were present.
    B. A new organization of employers and employees have been formed.
    C. One or the other of these men have been selected.
    D. The number of pages in the book is enough to discourage a reader.

44. The MOST accurate of the following sentences is:
    A. Between you and me, I think he is the better man.
    B. He was believed to be me.
    C. Is it us that you wish to see?
    D. The winners are him and her.

45. In the sentence, "The committee favored submiting the amendment to the electorate," the MISSPELLED word is
    A. committee B. submiting C. amendment D. electorate

46. In the sentence, "He maliciously demurred to an ajournment of the proceedings," the MISSPELLED word is
    A. maliciously B. demurred C. ajournment D. proceedings

47. In the sentence, "His innocence at that time is irrelevent in view of his more recent villainous demeanor," the MISSPELLED word is
    A. innocence B. irrelevent C. villainous D. demeanor

48. In the sentence, "The mischievous boys aggrevated the annoyance of their neighbor," the MISSPELLED word is
    A. mischievous B. aggrevated C. annoyance D. neighbor

49. In the sentence, "While his persiverance was commendable, his judgment was debatable, the MISSPELLED word is
    A. persiverance
    B. commendable
    C. judgment
    D. debatable

50. In the sentence, "He was hoping the appeal would facilitate his aquittal," the MISSPELLED word is
    A. hoping B. appeal C. facilitate D. aquittal

51. In the sentence, "It would be preferable for them to persue separate courses," the MISSPELLED word is
    A. preferable B. persue C. separate D. courses

52. In the sentence, "The litigant was complimented on his persistance and achievement," the MISSPELLED word is
    A. litigant
    B. complimented
    C. persistance
    D. achievement

53. In the sentence, "Ocassionally there are discrepancies in the descriptions of miscellaneous items," the MISSPELLED word is
    A. ocassionally
    B. discrepancies
    C. descriptions
    D. miscellaneous

54. In the sentence, "The councilmanic seargent-at-arms enforced the prohibition," the MISSPELLED word is
    A. councilmanic
    B. seargent-at-arms
    C. enforced
    D. prohibition

55. In the sentence, "The teacher had an ingenious device for mantaining attendance," the MISSPELLED word is
    A. ingenious B. device C. mantaining D. attendance

Questions 56-63.

DIRECTIONS: Questions 56 through 63 are to be answered on the basis of the following excerpt from a recorded annual report of the police department. This material should be read first and then referred to in answering these questions, which are to be answered SOLELY on the basis of the material herein contained.

LEGAL BUREAU

One of the more important functions of this bureau is to analyze and furnish the department with pertinent information concerning Federal and State statutes and Local Laws which affect the department, law enforcement or crime prevention. In addition, all measures introduced in the State Legislature and the City Council which may affect this department are carefully reviewed by members of the Legal Bureau and, where necessary, opinions and recommendations thereon are prepared.

Another important function of this office is the prosecution of cases in the Magistrate's Courts. This is accomplished by assignment of attorneys who are members of the Legal Bureau to appear in those cases which are deemed to raise issues of importance to the department or questions of law which require technical presentation to facilitate proper determination; and also in those cases where request is made for such appearances by a magistrate, some other official of the city, or a member of the force. Attorneys are regularly assigned to prosecute all cases in the Women's Court.

Proposed legislation was prepared and sponsored for introduction in the State Legislature and, at this writing, one of these proposals has already been enacted into law and five others are presently on the Governor's desk awaiting executive action. The new law prohibits the sale or possession of a hypodermic syringe or needle by an unauthorized person. The bureau's proposals awaiting executive action pertain to an amendment to the Code of Criminal Procedure prohibiting desk officers from taking bail in gambling cases or in cases mentioned in Section 552, Code of Criminal Procedure; including confidence men and swindlers as jostlers in the Penal Law; prohibiting the sale of switchblade knives of any size to children under 16 and bills extending the licensing period of gunsmiths.

The Legal Bureau has regularly cooperated with the Corporation Counsel and the District Attorneys in respect to matters affecting this department, and has continued to advise and represent the Police Athletic League, the Police Sports Association, the Police Relief Fund, and the Police Pension Fund.

The following is a statistical report of the activities of the bureau during the current year as compared with the previous year:

	Current Year	Previous Year
Memoranda of law prepared	68	83
Legal matters forwarded to corporation counsel	122	144
Letters requesting legal information	756	807
Letters requesting departmental records	139	111
Matters for publication	17	26
Court appearances of members of bureau	4,678	4,621
Conferences	94	103
Lectures at Police Academy	30	33
Reports on proposed legislation	194	255
Deciphering of codes	79	27
Expert testimony	31	16
Notices to court witnesses	55	81
Briefs prepared	22	18
Court papers prepared	258	--

56. One of the functions of the Legal Bureau is to
    A. review and make recommendations on proposed Federal laws affecting law enforcement
    B. prepare opinions on all measures introduced in the State Legislature and the City Council
    C. furnish the Police Department with pertinent information concerning all new Federal and State laws
    D. analyze all laws affecting the work of the Police Department

57. The one of the following that is NOT a function of the Legal Bureau is
    A. law enforcement and crime prevention
    B. prosecution of all cases in Women's Court
    C. advise and represent the Police Sports Association
    D. lecturing at the Police Academy

58. Members of the Legal Bureau frequently appear in Magistrate's Court for the purpose of
    A. defending members of the Police Force
    B. raising issues of importance to the Police Department
    C. prosecuting all offenders arrested by members of the Force
    D. facilitating proper determination of questions of law requiring technical presentation

59. The Legal Bureau sponsored a bill that would
    A. extend the licenses of gunsmiths
    B. prohibit the sale of switchblade knives to children of any size
    C. place confidence men and swindlers in the same category as jostlers in the Penal Law
    D. prohibit desk officers from admitting gamblers, confidence men, and swindlers to bail

60. From the report, it is NOT reasonable to infer that
   A. fewer bills affecting the Police Department were introduced in the current year
   B. the preparation of court papers was a new activity assumed in the current year
   C. the Code of Criminal Procedure authorizes desk officers to accept bail in certain cases
   D. the penalty for jostling and swindling is the same

61. According to the statistical report, the activity showing the GREATEST percentage of decrease in the current year as compared to the previous year was
   A. matters for publication
   B. reports on proposed legislation
   C. notices to court witnesses
   D. memoranda of law prepared

62. According to the statistical report, the activity showing the GREATEST percentage of increase in the current year as compare with the previous year was
   A. court appearances of members of the bureau
   B. giving expert testimony
   C. deciphering of codes
   D. letters requesting departmental records

63. According to the report, the percentage of bills prepared and sponsored by the Legal Bureau which were passed by the State Legislature and sent to the Governor for approval was APPROXIMATELY
   A. 3.1%
   B. 2.6%
   C. .5%
   D. not capable of determination from the data given

64. A squad of officers assigned to enforce a new parking regulation in a particular area issued tag summonses on a particular day as follows: four officers issued 16 summonses each; three issued 19 each; one issued 22; seven issued 25 each; eleven issued 28 each; ten issued 30 each; two issued 36 each; one issued 41; and three issued 45 each.
   The average number of summonses issued by a member of this squad was MOST NEARLY
   A. 6.2 B. 17.2 C. 21.0 D. 27.9

65. A water storage tank is 75 feet long and 30 feet wide and has a depth of 6½ feet. Each cubic foot of the tank holds 9½ gallons.
   The TOTAL capacity of the tank is _____ gallons.
   A. 73,125½ B. 131,625 C. 138,937½ D. 146,250

66. The price of admission to a PAL entertainment were $2.50 each for adults and $1.00 for children; the turnstile at the entrance showed that 358 persons entered and the gate receipts were $626.50.
The number of children who attended was
   A. 170   B. 175   C. 179   D. 183

66._____

67. A patrol car travels six times as fast as a bicycle.
If the patrol car goes 168 miles in two hours less time than the bicycle requires to go 42 miles, their respective rates of speed are _____ miles per hour.
   A. 36 and 6   B. 42 and 7   C. 63 and 10½   D. 126 and 21

67._____

68. The radiator of an automobile already contains six quarts of a 10% solution of alcohol.
In order to make a mixture of 20% alcohol, it will be necessary to add _____ quarts of alcohol.
   A. ¾   B. 1¾   C. 2½   D. 3

68._____

69. A man received an inheritance of $80,000 and wanted to invest it so that it would produce an annual income sufficient to pay his rent of $400 a month. In order to do this, he will have to receive interest or dividends at the rate of _____% per annum.
   A. 3   B. 4   C. 5¾   D. 6

69._____

70. If the price of a bus ticket varies *directly* as the mileage involved, and a ticket to travel 135 miles costs $29.70, a ticket for a 30-mile trip will cost
   A. $15.20   B. $13.40   C. $6.60   D. $2.20

70._____

71. A man owed a debt of $5,800. After a first payment of $100, he agreed to pay the balance by monthly payments in which each payment after this first would be $20 more than that of the preceding month.
If no interest charge is made, he will have to make, including the first payment, a total of _____ monthly payments.
   A. 16   B. 20   C. 24   D. 28

71._____

72. The written test of a civil service examination has a weight of 30, the oral test a weight of 20, experience a weight of 20, and the physical test a weight of 30. A candidate received ratings of 76 on the written test, 84 on the oral, and 80 for experience.
In order to attain an average of 85 on the examination, his rating on the physical test must be
   A. 86   B. 90   C. 94   D. 98

72._____

73. A family has an income of $3,200 per month. It spends 22% of this amount for rent, 36% for food, 16% for clothing, and 12% for additional household expenses. After meeting these expenses, 50% of the balance is deposited in the bank.
The amount deposited monthly is
   A. $224.00   B. $366.00   C. $448.00   D. $520.00

73._____

74. Upon retirement last July, an officer bought a farm of 64 acres for $18,000 per acre. He made a down payment of $612,000 and agreed to pay the balance in installments of $7,500 a month commencing on August 1, 2022. Disregarding interest, he will make his LAST payment in
    A. July 2028
    B. August 2030
    C. January 2032
    D. April 2035

75. 40% of those who commit a particular crime are subsequently arrested and convicted. 75% of those committed receive sentences of 10 years or more. Assuming that those arrested for the first time serve less than 10 years, the percentage of those committing this crime who receive sentences of ten years or more is MOST NEARLY
    A. 20%   B. 30%   C. 40%   D. 50%

KEY (CORRECT ANSWERS)

1.	A	21.	D	41.	A	61.	A
2.	D	22.	B	42.	C	62.	C
3.	A	23.	B	43.	D	63.	D
4.	A	24.	B	44.	A	64.	D
5.	C	25.	A	45.	B	65.	C
6.	B	26.	B	46.	C	66.	C
7.	C	27.	C	47.	C	67.	B
8.	B	28.	A	48.	B	68.	A
9.	A	29.	D	49.	A	69.	D
10.	C	30.	B	50.	D	70.	C
11.	C	31.	A	51.	B	71.	B
12.	A	32.	D	52.	C	72.	D
13.	A	33.	C	53.	A	73.	A
14.	B	34.	A	54.	B	74.	A
15.	B	35.	B	55.	C	75.	B
16.	D	36.	B	56.	D		
17.	A	37.	C	57.	A		
18.	A	38.	B	58.	D		
19.	C	39.	A	59.	C		
20.	A	40.	B	60.	D		

EXAMINATION SECTION

TEST 1

DIRECTIONS: Each question or incomplete statement is followed by several suggested answers or completions. Select the one that BEST answers the question or completes the statement. *PRINT THE LETTER OF THE CORRECT ANSWER IN THE SPACE AT THE RIGHT.*

1. Upon arriving at the scene of an accident in which a pedestrian was struck and killed by an automobile, an officer's first action was to clear the scene of spectators.
   Of the following, the PRINCIPAL reason for this action is that
   A. important evidence may be inadvertently destroyed by the crowd
   B. this is a fundamental procedure in first aid work
   C. the operator of the vehicle may escape in the crowd
   D. witnesses will speak more freely if other persons are not present

   1.____

2. In questioning witnesses, an officer is instructed to avoid leading questions or questions that will suggest the answer.
   Accordingly, when questioning a witness about the appearance of a suspect, it would be BEST for him to ask:
   A. What kind of hat did he wear?   B. Did he wear a felt hat?
   C. What did he wear?   D. Didn't he wear a hat?

   2.____

3. The only personal description the police have of a particular criminal was made several years ago.
   Of the following, the item in the description that will be MOST useful in identifying him at the present time is the
   A. color of his eyes   B. color of his hair
   C. number of teeth   D. weight

   3.____

4. Crime statistics indicate that property crimes such as larceny, burglary, and robbery are more numerous during winter months than in summer.
   The one of the following explanations that MOST adequately accounts for this situation is that
   A. human needs, such as clothing, food, heat, and shelter, are greater in winter
   B. criminal tendencies are aggravated by climatic changes
   C. there are more hours of darkness in winter and such crimes are usually committed under cover of darkness
   D. urban areas are more densely populated during winter months, affording greater opportunity for such crimes

   4.____

5. When automobile tire tracks are to be used as evidence, a plaster cast is made of them.
   Of the following, the MOST probable reason for taking a photograph is that
   A. photographs can be duplicated more easily than castings
   B. less skill is required for photographing than casting
   C. the tracks may be damaged in the casting process
   D. photographs are more easily transported than castings

6. It is generally recommended that an officer, in lifting a revolver that is to be sent to the police laboratory for ballistics tests and fingerprint examination, do so by insetting a pencil through the trigger guard rather than into the barrel of the weapon.
   The reason for preferring this procedure is that
   A. every precaution must be taken not to eliminate fingerprints on the weapon
   B. there is a danger of accidentally discharging the weapon by placing the pencil in the barrel
   C. the pencil may make scratches inside the barrel that will interfere with the ballistics tests
   D. a weapon can more easily be lifted by the trigger guard

7. PHYSICIAN is to PATIENT as ATTORNEY is to
   A. court   B. client   C. counsel   D. judge

8. JUDGE is to SENTENCE as JURY is to
   A. court   B. foreman   C. defendant   D. verdict

9. REVERSAL is to AFFIRMANCE as CONVICTION is to
   A. appeal   B. acquittal   C. error   D. mistrial

10. GENUINE is to TRUE as SPURIOUS is to
    A. correct   B. conceived   C. false   D. speculative

11. ALLEGIANCE is to LOYALTY as TREASON is to
    A. felony   B. faithful   C. obedience   D. rebellion

12. CONCUR is to AGREE as DIFFER is to
    A. coincide   B. dispute   C. join   D. repeal

13. A person who has an uncontrollable desire to steal without need is called a
    A. dipsomaniac   B. kleptomaniac
    C. monomaniac   D. pyromaniac

14. In the sentence, "The placing of any inflammable substance in any building or the placing of any device or contrivence capable of producing fire, for the purpose of causing a fire is an attempt to burn," the MISSPELLED word is
    A. inflammable   B. substance   C. device   D. contrivence

15. In the sentence, "The word 'break' also means obtaining an entrance into a building by any artifice used for that purpose, or by colussion with any person therein," the MISSPELLED word is
    A. obtaining   B. entrance   C. artifice   D. colussion

16. In the sentence, "Any person who with intent to provoke a breech of the peace causes a disturbance or is offensive to others may be deemed to have committed disorderly conduct," the MISSPELLED word is
    A. breech   B. disturbance   C. offensive   D. committed

17. In the sentence, "When the offender inflicts a grevious harm upon the person from whose possession, or in his presence, property is taken, he is guilty of robbery, the MISSPELLED word is
    A. offender   B. grevious   C. possession   D. presence

18. In the sentence, "A person who wilfully encourages or advises another person in attempting to take the latter's life is guilty of a felony," the MISSPELLED word is
    A. wilfully   B. encourages   C. advises   D. attempting

19. The treatment to be given the offender cannot alter the fact of his offense; but we can take measures to reduce the chances of similar acts in the future. We should banish the criminal, not in order to exact revenge nor directly to encourage reform, but to deter him and others from further illegal attacks on society.
    According to this paragraph, the PRINCIPAL reason for punishing criminals is to
    A. prevent the commission of future crimes
    B. remove them safely from society
    C. avenge society
    D. teach them that crime does not pay

20. Even the most comprehensive and best substantiated summaries of the total volume of criminal acts would not contribute greatly to an understanding of the varied social and biological factors which are sometimes assumed to enter into crime causation, nor would they indicate with any degree of precision the needs of police forces in combating crime.
    According to this statement,
    A. crime statistics alone do not determine the needs of police forces in combating crime
    B. crime statistics are essential to a proper understanding of the social factors of crime
    C. social and biological factor which enter the crime causation have little bearing on police needs
    D. a knowledge of the social and biological factors of crime is essential to a proper understanding of crime statistics

21. The police officer's art consists in applying and enforcing a multitude of laws and ordinances in such degree or proportion and in such manner that the greatest degree of social protection will be secured. The degree of enforcement and the method of application will vary with each neighborhood and community.
According to the foregoing paragraph,
    A. each neighborhood or community must judge for itself to what extent the law is to be enforced
    B. a police officer should only enforce those laws which are designed to give the greatest degree of social protection
    C. the manner and intensity of law enforcement is not necessarily the same in all communities
    D. all laws and ordinances must be enforced in a community with the same degree of intensity

22. Police control in the sense of regulating the details of police operations involves such matters as the technical means for so organizing the available personnel that competent police leadership, when secured, can operate effectively. It is concerned not so much with the extent to which popular controls can be trusted to guide and direct the course of police protection a with the administrative relationships which should exist between the component parts of the police organism.
According to the foregoing statement, police control is
    A. solely a matter of proper personnel assignment
    B. the means employed to guide and direct the course of police protection
    C. principally concerned with the administrative relationships between units of a police organization
    D. the sum total of means employed in rendering police protection

23. Two patrol cars hurry to the scene of an accident from different directions. The first proceeds at the rate of 45 miles per hour and arrives in four minutes. Although the second car travels over a route which is three-fourths of a mile longer, it arrives at the scene only a half-minute later.
The speed of the second car, expressed in miles per hour, is
    A. 50   B. 55   C. 60   D. 65

24. A motorcycle officer issued 72 traffic summonses in January, 60 in February and 83 in March.
In order to average 75 summonses per month for the four months of January, February, March, and April, during April he will have to issue _____ summonses.
    A. 80   B. 85   C. 90   D. 95

25. In a unit of the Police Department to which 40 officers are assigned, the sick report record during 2022 was as follows: 1 was absent 8 days, 5 were absent 3 days each, 4 were absent 5 days each, 10 were absent 2 days each, 8 were absent 4 days each, 5 were absent 1 day each.
The average number of days on sick report for all the members of this unit is MOST NEARLY
    A. ½   B. 1   C. 2 ½   D. 3

Questions 26-30.

DIRECTIONS: Column I lists various statements of fact. Column II is a list of crimes. Next to the numbers corresponding to the number preceding the statements of fact in Column I, place the letter preceding the crime listed in Column II with which Jones should be charged. In answering these questions, the following definitions of crimes should be applied, bearing in mind that ALL elements contained in the definitions must be present in order to charge a person with that crime.

BURGLARY is breaking and entering a building with intent to commit some crime therein. EMBEZZLEMENT is the appropriation to one's use of another's property which has been entrusted to one's care or which has come lawfully into one's possession. EXTORTION is taking or obtaining property from another with his consent, induced by a wrongful use of force or fear. LARCENY is taking and carrying away the personal property of another with intent to deprive or defraud the true owner of the use and benefit of such property. ROBBERY is the unlawful taking of the personal property of another from his person or in his presence by force or violence, or fear of injury.

COLUMN I

26. Jones, believing Smith had induced his wife to leave him, went to Smith's home armed with a knife with which he intended to assault Smith. When his knock was unanswered, he forced open the door of Smith's home and entered but, finding the house empty, he threw away the knife and left.

27. Jones was employed as a collection agent by Smith. When Smith refused to reimburse him for certain expenses he claimed to have incurred in connection with his work, Jones deducted this amount from sums he had collected for Smith.

28. Jones spent the night in a hotel. During the night he left his room, went downstairs to the desk, stole money and returned to his room.

29. Jones, a building inspector, found that the elevators in Smith's building were being operated without a permit. He threatened to report the matter and have the elevators shut down unless Smith paid him a sum of money. Smith paid the amount demanded

30. Jones held-up Smith on the street and, pointing a revolve at him, demanded his money. Smith, without resisting, handed Jones his money. When Jones was apprehended, it was discovered that the revolver was a toy.

COLUMN II

A. burglary
B. embezzlement
C. extortion
D. larceny
E. robbery
F. no crime

26.____
27.____
28.____
29.____
30.____

Questions 31-40.

DIRECTIONS: Questions 31 through 40 consist of statements from which a term is missing. Each of these statements can be completed correctly with one of the terms in the following list. In the space opposite the number corresponding to the number of the question, place the LETTER preceding the term in the following list which MOST accurately completes the statement.

    A. affidavit
    B. appeal
    C. arraignment
    D. arrest
    E. bench warrant
    F. habeas corpus
    G. indictment
    H. injunction
    I. sentence
    J. subpoena

31. A _____ is a writ calling witnesses to court.   31._____

32. _____ is a method used to obtain a review of a case in court of superior jurisdiction.   32._____

33. A judgment passed by a court on a person on trial as a criminal offender is called a _____.   33._____

34. _____ is a writ or order requiring a person to refrain from a particular act.   34._____

35. _____ is the name given to a writ commanding the bringing of the body of a certain person before a certain court.   35._____

36. A _____ is a court order directing that an offender be brought into court.   36._____

37. The calling of a defendant before the court to answer an accusation is called _____.   37._____

38. The accusation in writing, presented by the grand jury to a competent court charging a person with a public offense is an _____.   38._____

39. A sworn declaration in writing is an _____.   39._____

40. _____ is the taking of a person into custody for the purpose of holding him to answer a criminal charge.   40._____

Questions 41-55.

DIRECTIONS: Questions 41 through 55 consist of statements from which a term is missing. Each of these statements can be completed correctly with one of the terms in the following list. In the space opposite the number corresponding to the number of the question, place the LETTER preceding the term in the following list which MOST accurately completes the statement.

A.	accessory	B.	accomplice	C.	alibi
D.	autopsy	E.	ballistics	F.	capital
G.	confidence man	H.	commission	I.	conspiracy
J.	corroborated	K.	grand jury	L.	homicide
M.	misdemeanors	N.	penology	O.	perjury

41. _____ is the dissection of a dead human body to determine the cause of death. 41._____

42. The general term which mean the killing of one person by another is _____. 42._____

43. _____ is the science of the punishment of crime. 43._____

44. False swearing constitutes the crime of _____. 44._____

45. A combination of two or more persons to accomplish a criminal or unlawful act is called _____. 45._____

46. By _____ is meant evidence showing that a defendant was in another place when the crime was committed. 46._____

47. _____ is a term frequently used to describe a person engaged in a kind of swindling operation. 47._____

48. A _____ offense is one for which a life sentence or death penalty is prescribed by law. 48._____

49. A violation of a law may be either an act of omission or an act of _____. 49._____

50. An _____ is a person who is liable to prosecution for the identical offense charged against a defendant on trial. 50._____

51. A person would be an _____ who after the commission of a crime aided in the escape of one he knew to be an offender. 51._____

52. An official body called to hear complaints and to determine whether there is ground for criminal prosecution is known as the _____. 52._____

53. Crimes are generally divided into two classes, namely felonies and _____. 53._____

54. _____ is the science of the motion of projectiles. 54._____

55. Testimony of a witness which is confirmed by another witness is _____. 55._____

Questions 56-60.

DIRECTIONS: Next to the question number which corresponds with the number of each item in Column I, place the letter preceding the adjective in Column II which BEST describes the persons in Column I.

COLUMN I	COLUMN II	
56. A talkative woman	A. abstemious	56.____
	B. pompous	
57. A person on a reducing diet	C. erudite	57.____
	D. benevolent	
58. A scholarly professor	E. docile	58.____
	F. loquacious	
59. A man who seldom speaks	G. indefatigable	59.____
	H. taciturn	
60. A charitable person		60.____

Questions 61-65.

DIRECTIONS: Next to the question number which corresponds with the number preceding each profession in Column I, place the letter preceding the word in Column II which BEST explains the subject of that profession.

COLUMN I	COLUMN II	
61. Geologist	A. animals	61.____
	B. eyes	
62. Oculist	C. feet	62.____
	D. fortune-telling	
63. Podiatrist	E. language	63.____
	F. rocks	
64. Palmist	G. stamps	64.____
	H. woman	
65. Zoologist		65.____

Questions 66-70.

DIRECTIONS: Next to the question number corresponding to the number of each of the words in Column I, place the letter preceding the word in Column II that is MOST NEARLY OPPOSITE to it in meaning.

COLUMN I	COLUMN II	
66. comely	A. beautiful	66.____
	B. cowardly	
67. eminent	C. kind	67.____
	D. sedate	
68. frugal	E. shrewd	68.____
	F. ugly	
69. gullible	G. unknown	69.____
	H. wasteful	
70. valiant		70.____

KEY (CORRECT ANSWERS)

1.	A	16.	A	31.	J	46.	C	61.	F
2.	C	17.	B	32.	B	47.	G	62.	B
3.	A	18.	A	33.	I	48.	F	63.	C
4.	C	19.	A	34.	H	49.	H	64.	D
5.	C	20.	A	35.	F	50.	B	65.	A
6.	C	21.	C	36.	E	51.	A	66.	F
7.	B	22.	C	37.	C	52.	L	67.	G
8.	D	23.	A	38.	G	53.	N	68.	H
9.	B	24.	B	39.	A	54.	E	69.	E
10.	C	25.	C	40.	D	55.	K	70.	B
11.	D	26.	A	41.	D	56.	F		
12.	B	27.	B	42.	M	57.	A		
13.	B	28.	D	43.	O	58.	C		
14.	D	29.	C	44.	P	59.	H		
15.	D	30.	E	45.	J	60.	D		

EXAMINATION SECTION
TEST 1

DIRECTIONS: Each question or incomplete statement is followed by several suggested answers or completions. Select the one that BEST answers the question or completes the statement. *PRINT THE LETTER OF THE CORRECT ANSWER IN THE SPACE AT THE RIGHT.*

1. The *only* states that have not enacted the Uniform Criminal Extradition Act are

    A. Georgia and Louisiana
    B. South Carolina and Mississippi
    C. Alabama and Georgia
    D. Alabama and South Carolina

2. With respect to the procedures involved in arresting and returning fugitives to the state in which the crime was committed, which of the following statements is INCORRECT?

    A. An extradition warrant is a warrant issued by the governor of the state seeking the return of a fugitive.
    B. A rendition warrant is a warrant issued by the governor of the state where the fugitive is located now.
    C. The guilt or innocence of the fugitive is not a matter of concern to the officials of the state where the fugitive is located, except if it bears on the identity of such person.
    D. If the governor decides to issue a rendition warrant, it must be directed for execution to a police officer.

3. If a police officer executes a rendition warrant and then gives custody of the fugitive to an agent of the demanding state before bringing said fugitive before a judge of a court of record, the police officer commits

    A. official misconduct
    B. a felony
    C. a non-criminal civil rights violation
    D. no offense under the law

4. The Federal Fugitive Felony Act is a means by which the F.B.I, and the U.S. Marshal can cooperate in bringing about the capture of a felon wanted in this state. In order to obtain this assistance, certain conditions must be met.
Which of the following is NOT a properly stated condition?

    A. Facts must be shown that the felon has crossed state lines or left the country.
    B. A felony warrant must be outstanding in this state.
    C. The federal authorities must agree to bear the expense of return.
    D. The F.B.I, or the U.S. Marshall must be requested to assist in the matter.

5. Lt. Smith is approached by a police officer from San Diego who tells him he knows the whereabouts of a person who is wanted for homicide in California. Lt. Smith determines that the governor has issued a Governor's Warrant of Extradition. He takes the suspect into custody and delivers him to the police officer from California for return thereto. Lt. Smith has committed

    A. a felony B. a misdemeanor
    C. a violation D. no offense

6. If a violation of the criminal provisions of the Federal Civil Rights Act occurs, the agency that should be notified immediately is the

   A. Department of Justice
   B. F.B.I.
   C. Department of State
   D. Human Rights Commission

7. Which of the following statements is INCORRECT?

   A. Arrests for criminal violations of the U.S. Code concerning civil rights should be made by the F.B.I.
   B. When you have witnessed a criminal violation of the civil rights provisions of STATE law, an arrest may be made without a warrant.
   C. When you have not witnessed the offense as in Choice B, you should arrest if it is a crime but not arrest if it is a violation.
   D. Police officers should take summary action ONLY when there has been a criminal violation of state law.

Questions 8 to 25.

DIRECTIONS: Each question consists of a statement. You are to indicate whether the statement is TRUE (T) or FALSE (F). *PRINT THE LETTER OF THE CORRECT ANSWER IN THE SPACE AT THE RIGHT.*

Questions 8 to 14 refer to the following statement.
On January 17, 2007, the Governor of New Jersey properly demanded that Steven, a wanted felon under New Jersey law, be delivered over to an agent of New Jersey and returned to that state. All necessary supporting documents (affidavits, copies of warrants or judgments of conviction, etc.) and required information are contained in the demand from the New Jersey Governor. The New York Governor, in response to the demand, signs and seals a warrant of arrest for Steven.

8. The warrant of arrest issued by the New York Governor may be directed to any police officer.

9. The warrant of arrest issued by the New York Governor may be directed to any person the Governor thinks fit to execute it.

10. Even if a non-police officer is chosen to execute the warrant, he shall have the authority to command assistance in executing it.

11. If a non-police officer executing the Governor"s warrant commands assistance and the person refuses, no offense has been committed.

12. Any person arrested under the authority of a governor's warrant shall be brought before a judge or justice of a court of record.

13. If the arrested person is brought before a judge or justice of a court of record, said judge or justice shall inform the arrested person of his right to counsel.

14. Any officer who delivers the person arrested under a governor's warrant to the agent of a demanding state without first bringing the person before a judge or justice of a court of record commits a felony. 14._____

Questions 15 to 25 refer to the following statement.

Samuel, a credible person, under oath before a local criminal court in this state, charges Steven with having committed a crime in New Jersey and with having fled from justice in New Jersey.

15. The judge of the local criminal court can issue a warrant of arrest for Steven. 15._____

16. If a warrant of arrest is issued on the above facts, it may be addressed to any police officer, any peace officer, or any person deemed fit by the judge to execute it. 16._____

17. If a warrant of arrest is issued, the person, if arrested, MUST be brought before the court which issues the warrant. 17._____

18. The information given to the court by Samuel is sufficient to authorize an arrest without a warrant by any police officer or private person. 18._____

19. The previous statement would be TRUE if reasonable information had been given that Steven stands charged in New Jersey with a crime punishable by either death or a term of imprisonment exceeding one year. 19._____

20. If Steven is arrested without a warrant for a New Jersey crime, he must be brought with all practical speed before a judge or justice of a court of record in this state. 20._____

21. If Steven is arrested without a warrant in a proper case for an offense committed in New Jersey, the judge MUST, by a warrant reciting the accusation, commit Steven to the county jail for NOT MORE than 30 days. 21._____

22. The reason for the time period in the above statement is to enable an arrest of Steven to be made by virtue of a governor's warrant. 22._____

23. In any event, if Steven is taken into custody and brought before a local criminal court of this state, he may be admitted to bail by the local criminal court. 23._____

24. In the event Steven is arrested without a warrant for a New Jersey crime and is held for NOT MORE than 30 days, that period of detention may be extended by NOT MORE than an aggregate of 60 days if he is not arrested under a governor's warrant within the original 30 days. 24._____

25. Except as it may be necessary for identification purposes, the guilt or innocence of Steven may NOT be inquired into by the Governor of New York. 25._____

KEY (CORRECT ANSWERS)

1.	B	11.	F
2.	D	12.	T
3.	B	13.	T
4.	C	14.	T
5.	A	15.	T
6.	B	16.	F
7.	C	17.	F
8.	T	18.	F
9.	T	19.	T
10.	T	20.	F

21. T
22. T
23. F
24. T
25. T

READING COMPREHENSION
UNDERSTANDING AND INTERPRETING WRITTEN MATERIAL
EXAMINATION SECTION
TEST 1

DIRECTIONS: Each question or incomplete statement is followed by several suggested answers or completions. Select the one that BEST answers the question or completes the statement. *PRINT THE LETTER OF THE CORRECT ANSWER IN THE SPACE AT THE RIGHT.*

Questions 1-4.

DIRECTIONS: Questions 1 through 4 are to be answered SOLELY on the basis of the following passage.

Those engaged in the exercise of First Amendment rights by pickets, marches, parades, and open-air assemblies are not exempted from obeying valid local traffic ordinances. In a recent pronouncement, Mr. Justice Baxter, speaking for the Supreme Court, wrote:

The rights of free speech and assembly, while fundamental to our democratic society, still do not mean that everyone with opinions or beliefs to express may address a group at any public place and at any time. The constitutional guarantee of liberty implies the existence of an organized society maintaining public order, without which liberty itself would be lost in the excesses of anarchy. The control of travel on the streets is a clear example of governmental responsibility to insure this necessary order. A restriction in that relation, designed to promote the public convenience in the interest of all, and not susceptible to abuses of discriminatory application, cannot be disregarded by the attempted exercise of some civil rights which, in other circumstances, would be entitled to protection. One would not be justified in ignoring the familiar red light because this was thought to be a means of social protest. Governmental authorities have the duty and responsibility to keep their streets open and available for movement. A group of demonstrators could not insist upon the right to cordon off a street, or entrance to a public or private building, and allow no one to pass who did not agree to listen to their exhortations.

1. Which of the following statements BEST reflects Mr. Justice Baxter's view of the relationship between liberty and public order?   1._____

    A. Public order cannot exist without liberty.
    B. Liberty cannot exist without public order.
    C. The existence of liberty undermines the existence of public order.
    D. The maintenance of public order insures the existence of liberty.

2. According to the above passage, local traffic ordinances result from   2._____

    A. governmental limitations on individual liberty
    B. governmental responsibility to insure public order
    C. majority rule as determined by democratic procedures
    D. restrictions on expression of dissent

3. The above passage suggests that government would be acting improperly if a local traffic ordinance

   A. was enforced in a discriminatory manner
   B. resulted in public inconvenience
   C. violated the right of free speech and assembly
   D. was not essential to public order

4. Of the following, the MOST appropriate title for the above passage is

   A. THE RIGHTS OF FREE SPEECH AND ASSEMBLY
   B. ENFORCEMENT OF LOCAL TRAFFIC ORDINANCES
   C. FIRST AMENDMENT RIGHTS AND LOCAL TRAFFIC ORDINANCES
   D. LIBERTY AND ANARCHY

Questions 5-8

DIRECTIONS: Questions 5 through 8 are to be answered SOLELY on the basis of the following passage

On November 8, 1976, the Supreme Court refused to block the payment of Medicaid funds for elective abortions. The Court's action means that a new Federal statute that bars the use of Federal funds for abortions unless abortion is necessary to save the life of the mother will not go into effect for many months, if at all.

A Federal District Court in Brooklyn ruled the following month that the statute was unconstitutional and ordered that Federal reimbursement for the costs of abortions continue on the same basis as reimbursements for the costs of pregnancy and childbirth-related services.

Technically, what the Court did today was to deny a request by Senator Howard Ramsdell and others for a stay blocking enforcement of the District Court order pending appeal. The Court's action was a victory for New York City. The City's Health and Hospitals Corporation initiated one of the two lawsuits challenging the new statute that led to the District Court's decision. The Corporation also opposed the request for a Supreme Court stay of that decision, telling the Court in a memorandum that a stay would subject the Corporation to a *grave and irreparable injury*.

5. According to the above passage, it would be CORRECT to state that the Health and Hospitals Corporation

   A. joined Senator Ramsdell in his request for a stay
   B. opposed the statute which limited reimbursement for the cost of abortions
   C. claimed that it would experience a loss if the District Court order was enforced
   D. appealed the District Court decision

6. The above passage indicates that the Supreme Court acted in DIRECT response to

   A. a lawsuit initiated by the Health and Hospitals Corporation
   B. a ruling by a Federal District Court
   C. a request for a stay
   D. the passage of a new Federal statute

7. According to the above passage, it would be CORRECT to state that the Supreme Court

   A. blocked enforcement of the District Court order
   B. refused a request for a stay to block enforcement of the Federal statute
   C. ruled that the new Federal statute was unconstitutional
   D. permitted payment of Federal funds for abortion to continue

8. Following are three statements concerning abortion that might be correct:
   I. Abortion costs are no longer to be Federally reimbursed on the same basis as those for pregnancy and childbirth
   II. Federal funds have not been available for abortions except to save the life of the mother
   III. Medicaid has paid for elective abortions in the past

   According to the passage above, which of the following CORRECTLY classifies the above statements into those that are true and those that are not true?

   A. I is true, but II and III are not.
   B. I and III are true, but II is not.
   C. I and II are true, but III is not.
   D. III is true, but I and II are not.

Questions 9-12.

DIRECTIONS: Questions 9 through 12 are to be answered SOLELY on the basis of the following passage.

A person may use physical force upon another person when and to the extent he reasonably believes such to be necessary to defend himself or a third person from what he reasonably believes to be the use or imminent use of unlawful physical force by such other person, unless (a) the latter's conduct was provoked by the actor himself with intent to cause physical injury to another person; or (b) the actor was the initial aggressor; or (c) the physical force involved is the product of a combat by agreement not specifically authorized by law.

A person may not use deadly physical force upon another person under the circumstances specified above unless (a) he reasonably believes that such other person is using or is about to use deadly physical force. Even in such case, however, the actor may not use deadly physical force if he knows he can, with complete safety, as to himself and others avoid the necessity of doing so by retreating; except that he is under no duty to retreat if he is in his dwelling and is not the initial aggressor; or (b) he reasonably believes that such other person is committing or attempting to commit a kidnapping, forcible rape, or forcible sodomy.

9. Jones and Smith, who have not met before, get into an argument in a tavern. Smith takes a punch at Jones, but misses. Jones then hits Smith on the chin with his fist. Smith falls to the floor and suffers minor injuries.
   According to the above passage, it would be CORRECT to state that _____ justified in using physical force.

   A. only Smith was   B. only Jones was
   C. both Smith and Jones were   D. neither Smith nor Jones was

10. While walking down the street, Brady observes Miller striking Mrs. Adams on the head with his fist in an attempt to steal her purse.
According to the above passage, it would be CORRECT to state that Brady would

    A. not be justified in using deadly physical force against Miller since Brady can safely retreat
    B. be justified in using physical force against Miller but not deadly physical force
    C. not be justified in using physical force against Miller since Brady himself is not being attacked
    D. be justified in using deadly physical force

11. Winters is attacked from behind by Sharp, who attempts to beat up Winters with a blackjack. Winters disarms Sharp and succeeds in subduing him with a series of blows to the head. Sharp stops fighting and explains that he thought Winters was the person who had robbed his apartment a few minutes before, but now realizes his mistake.
According to the above passage, it would be CORRECT to state that

    A. Winters was justified in using physical force on Sharp only to the extent necessary to defend himself
    B. Winters was not justified in using physical force on Sharp since Sharp's attack was provoked by what he believed to be Winters' behavior
    C. Sharp was justified in using physical force on Winters since he reasonably believed that Winters had unlawfully robbed him
    D. Winters was justified in using physical force on Sharp only because Sharp was acting mistakenly in attacking him

12. Roberts hears a noise in the cellar of his home, and, upon investigation, discovers an intruder, Welch. Welch moves towards Roberts in a threatening manner, thrusts his hand into a bulging pocket, and withdraws what appears to be a gun. Roberts thereupon strikes Welch over the head with a golf club. He then sees that the *gun* is a toy. Welch later dies of head injuries. According to the above passage, it would be CORRECT to state that Roberts was

    A. justified in using deadly physical force because he reasonably believed Welch was about to use deadly physical force
    B. not justified in using deadly physical force
    C. justified in using deadly physical force only because he did not provoke Welch's conduct
    D. justified in using deadly physical force only because he was not the initial aggressor

Questions 13-16.

DIRECTIONS: Questions 13 through 16 are to be answered SOLELY on the basis of the following passage.

From the beginning, the Supreme Court has supervised the fairness of trials conducted by the Federal government. But the Constitution, as originally drafted, gave the court no such general authority in state cases. The court's power to deal with state cases comes from the Fourteenth Amendment, which became part of the Constitution in 1868. The crucial provision forbids any state to *deprive any person of life, liberty, or property without due process of law.*

The guarantee of *due process* would seem, at the least, to require fair procedure in criminal trials. But curiously the Supreme Court did not speak on the question for many decades. During that time, however, the due process clause was interpreted to bar *unreasonable* state economic regulations, such as minimum wage laws.

In 1915, there came the case of Leo M. Frank, a Georgian convicted of murder in a trial that he contended was dominated by mob hysteria. Historians now agree that there was such hysteria, with overtones of anti-semitism.

The Supreme Court held that it could not look past the findings of the Georgia courts that there had been no mob atmosphere at the trial. Justices Oliver Wendell Holmes and Charles Evans Hughes dissented, arguing that the constitutional guarantee would be *a barren one* if the Federal courts could not make their own inferences from the facts.

In 1923, the case of Moore v. Dempsey involved five Arkansas Blacks convicted of murder and sentenced to death in a community so aroused against them that at one point they were saved from lynching only by Federal troops. Witnesses against them were said to have been beaten into testifying.

The court, though not actually setting aside the convictions, directed a lower Federal court to hold a habeas corpus hearing to find out whether the trial had been fair, or whether the whole proceeding had been *a mask—that counsel, jury, and judge were swept to the fatal end by an irresistible wave of public passion.*

13. According to the above passage, the Supreme Court's INITIAL interpretation of the Fourteenth Amendment

    A. protected state supremacy in economic matters
    B. increased the scope of Federal jurisdiction
    C. required fair procedures in criminal trials
    D. prohibited the enactment of minimum wage laws

14. According to the above passage, the Supreme Court in the Frank case

    A. denied that there had been mob hysteria at the trial
    B. decided that the guilty verdict was supported by the evidence
    C. declined to question the state court's determination of the facts
    D. found that Leo Frank had not received *due process*

15. According to the above passage, the dissenting judges in the Frank case maintained that

    A. due process was an empty promise in the circumstances of that case
    B. the Federal courts could not guarantee certain provisions of the Constitution
    C. the Federal courts should not make their own inferences from the facts in state cases
    D. the Supreme Court had rendered the Constitution *barren*

16. Of the following, the MOST appropriate title for the above passage is

    A. THE CONDUCT OF FEDERAL TRIALS
    B. THE DEVELOPMENT OF STATES' RIGHTS: 1868-1923
    C. MOORE V. DEMPSEY: A CASE STUDY IN CRIMINAL JUSTICE
    D. DUE PROCESS-THE EVOLUTION OF A CONSTITUTIONAL CORNERSTONE

Questions 17-20.

DIRECTIONS: Questions 17 through 20 are to be answered SOLELY on the basis of the following passage.

The difficulty experienced in determining which party has the burden of proving payment or non-payment is due largely to a lack of consistency between the rules of pleading and the rules of proof. In some cases, a plaintiff is obligated by a rule of pleading to allege non-payment on his complaint, yet is not obligated to prove non-payment on the trial. An action upon a contract for the payment of money will serve as an illustration. In such a case, the plaintiff must allege non-payment in his complaint, but the burden of proving payment on the trial is upon the defendant. An important and frequently cited case on this problem is Conkling v. Weatherwax. In that case, the action was brought to establish and enforce a legacy as a lien upon real property. The defendant alleged in her answer that the legacy had been paid. There was no witness competent to testify for the plaintiff to show that the legacy had not been paid. Therefore, the question of the burden of proof became of primary importance since, if the plaintiff had the burden of proving non-payment, she must fail in her action; whereas if the burden of proof was on the defendant to prove payment, the plaintiff might win. The Court of Appeals held that the burden of proof was on the plaintiff. In the course of his opinion, Judge Vann attempted to harmonize the conflicting cases on this subject, and for that purpose formulated three rules. These rules have been construed and applied to numerous subsequent cases. As so construed and applied, these may be summarized as follows:

Rule 1. In an action upon a contract for the payment of money only, where the complaint does not allege a balance due over and above all payments made, the plaintiff must allege nonpayment in his complaint, but the burden of proving payment is upon the defendant. In such a case, payment is an affirmative defense which the defendant must plead in his answer. If the defendant fails to plead payment, but pleads a general denial instead, he will not be permitted to introduce evidence of payment.

Rule 2. Where the complaint sets forth a balance in excess of all payments, owing to the structure of the pleading, burden is upon the plaintiff to prove his allegation. In this case, the defendant is not required to plead payment as a defense in his answer but may introduce evidence of payment under a general denial.

Rule 3. When the action is not upon contract for the payment of money, but is upon an obligation created by operation of law, or is for the enforcement of a lien where non-payment of the amount secured is part of the cause of action, it is necessary both to allege and prove the fact of nonpayment.

17. In the above passage, the case of Conkling v. Weatherwax was cited PRIMARILY to illustrate   17.____

    A. a case where the burden of proof was on the defendant to prove payment
    B. how the question of the burden of proof can affect the outcome of a case
    C. the effect of a legacy as a lien upon real property
    D. how conflicting cases concerning the burden of proof were harmonized

18. According to the above passage, the pleading of payment is a defense in Rule(s)   18.____

    A. 1, but not Rules 2 and 3
    B. 2, but not Rules 1 and 3
    C. 1 and 3, but not Rule 2
    D. 2 and 3, but not Rule 1

19. The facts in Conkling v. Weatherwax CLOSELY resemble the conditions described in   19.____

    A. Rule #1
    B. Rule #2
    C. Rule #3
    D. none of the rules

20. The MAJOR topic of the above passage may BEST be described as   20.____

    A. determining the ownership of property
    B. providing a legal definition
    C. placing the burden of proof
    D. formulating rules for deciding cases

Questions 21-25.

DIRECTIONS: Questions 21 through 25 are to be answered SOLELY on the basis of the following passage.

The law is quite clear that evidence obtained in violation of Section 605 of the Federal Communications Act is not admissible in Federal court. However, the law as to the admissibility of evidence in state court is far from clear. Had the Supreme Court of the United States made the wiretap exclusionary rule applicable to the states, such confusion would not exist.

In the case of Alton v. Texas, the Supreme Court was called upon to determine whether wiretapping by state and local officers came within the proscription of the Federal statute and, if so, whether Section 605 required the same remedies for its vindication in state courts. In answer to the first question, Mr. Justice Minton, speaking for the court, flatly stated that Section 605 made it a federal crime for anyone to intercept telephone messages and divulge what he learned. The court went on to say that a state officer who testified in state court concerning the existence, contents, substance, purport, effect, or meaning of an intercepted conversation violated the Federal law and committed a criminal act. In regard to the second question, how-ever, the Supreme Court felt constrained by due regard for federal-state relations to answer in the negative. Mr. Justice Minton stated that the court would not presume, in the absence of a clear manifestation of congressional intent, that Congress intended to supersede state rules of evidence.

Because the Supreme Court refused to apply the exclusionary rule to wiretap evidence that was being used in state courts, the states respectively made this decision for themselves. According to hearings held before a congressional committee in 1975, six states authorize wiretapping by statute, 33 states impose total bans on wiretapping, and 11 states have no definite statute on the subject. For examples of extremes, a statute in Pennsylvania will be compared with a statute in New York.

The Pennsylvania statute provides that no communications by telephone or telegraph can be intercepted without permission of both parties. It also specifically prohibits such interception by public officials and provides that evidence obtained cannot be used in court.

The lawmakers in New York, recognizing the need for legal wire-tapping, authorized wiretapping by statute. A New York law authorizes the issuance of an ex parte order upon oath or affirmation for limited wiretapping. The aim of the New York law is to allow court-ordered wiretapping and to encourage the testimony of state officers concerning such wiretapping in court. The New York law was found to be constitutional by the New York State Supreme Court in 1975. Other states, including Oregon, Maryland, Nevada, and Massachusetts, enacted similar laws which authorize court-ordered wiretapping.

To add to this legal disarray, the vast majority of the states, including New Jersey and New York, permit wiretapping evidence to be received in court even though obtained in violation of the state laws and of Section 605 of the Federal act. However, some states, such as Rhode Island, have enacted statutory exclusionary rules which provide that illegally procured wiretap evidence is incompetent in civil as well as criminal actions.

21. According to the above passage, a state officer who testifies in New York State court concerning the contents of a conversation he overheard through a court-ordered wire-tap is in violation of _____ law.

    A. state law but not federal
    B. federal law but not state
    C. federal law and state
    D. neither federal nor state

22. According to the above passage, which of the following statements concerning states statutes on wiretapping is CORRECT?

    A. The number of states that impose total bans on wiretapping is three times as great as the number of states with no definite statute on wiretapping.
    B. The number of states having no definite statute on wiretapping is more than twice the number of states authorizing wiretapping.
    C. The number of states which authorize wiretapping by statute and the number of states having no definite statute on wiretapping exceed the number of states imposing total bans on wiretapping.
    D. More states authorize wiretapping by statute than impose total bans on wiretapping.

23. Following are three statements concerning wiretapping that might be valid:
    I. In Pennsylvania, only public officials may legally intercept telephone communications.
    II. In Rhode Island, evidence obtained through an illegal wiretap is incompetent in criminal, but not civil, actions.
    III. Neither Massachusetts nor Pennsylvania authorizes wiretapping by public officials.

    According to the above passage, which of the following CORRECTLY classifies these statements into those that are valid and those that are not?

    A. I is valid, but II and III are not.
    B. II is valid, but I and III are not.
    C. II and III are valid, but I is not.
    D. None of the statements is valid.

24. According to the above passage, evidence obtained in violation of Section 605 of the Federal Communications Act is inadmissible in

    A. federal court but not in any state courts
    B. federal court and all state courts
    C. all state courts but not in federal court
    D. federal court and some state courts

25. In regard to state rules of evidence, Mr. Justice Minton expressed the Court's opinion that Congress

    A. intended to supersede state rules of evidence, as manifested by Section 605 of the Federal Communications Act
    B. assumed that federal statutes would govern state rules of evidence in all wiretap cases
    C. left unclear whether it intended to supersede state rules of evidence
    D. precluded itself from superseding state rules of evidence through its regard for federal-state relations

KEY (CORRECT ANSWERS)

1. B
2. B
3. A
4. C
5. B

6. C
7. D
8. D
9. B
10. B

11. A
12. A
13. D
14. C
15. A

16. D
17. B
18. A
19. C
20. C

21. B
22. A
23. D
24. D
25. C

TEST 2

DIRECTIONS: Each question or incomplete statement is followed by several suggested answers or completions. Select the one that BEST answers the question or completes the Statement. *PRINT THE LETTER OF THE CORRECT ANSWER IN THE SPACE AT THE RIGHT.*

Questions 1-3.

DIRECTIONS: Questions 1 through 3 are to be answered SOLELY on the basis of the following passage.

The State Assembly has passed a bill that would require all state agencies, public authorities, and local governments to refuse bids in excess of $2,000 from any foreign firm or corporation. The only exceptions to this outright prohibition against public buying of foreign goods or services would be for products not available in this country, goods of a quality unobtainable from an American supplier, and products using foreign materials that are *substantially* manufactured in the United States.

This bill is a flagrant violation of the United States' officially espoused trade principles. It would add to the costs of state and local governments. It could provoke retaliatory action from many foreign governments against the state and other American producers, and foreign governments would be fully entitled to take such retaliatory action under the General Agreement on Tariffs and Trade, which the United States has signed.

The State Senate, which now has the Assembly bill before it, should reject this protectionist legislation out of enlightened regard for the interests of the taxpayers and producers of the State—as well as for those of the nation and its trading partners generally. In this time of unemployment and international monetary disorder, the State—with its reputation for intelligent and progressive law-making—should avoid contributing to what could become a tidal wave of protectionism here and overseas.

1. Under the requirements of the bill passed by the State Assembly, a bid from a foreign manufacturer in excess of $2,000 can be accepted by a state agency or local government only if it meets which one of the following requirements?
The

   A. bid is approved individually by the State Legislature
   B. bidder is willing to accept payment in United States currency
   C. bid is for an item of a quality unobtainable from an American supplier
   D. bid is for an item which would be more expensive if it were purchased from an American supplier

1._____

2. The author of the above passage feels that the bill passed by the State Assembly should be

   A. passed by the State Senate and put into effect
   B. passed by the State Senate but vetoed by the Governor
   C. reintroduced into the State Assembly and rejected
   D. rejected by the State Senate

2._____

3. The author of the above passage calls the practice of prohibiting purchase of products manufactured by foreign countries

   A. prohibition
   B. protectionism
   C. retaliatory action
   D. isolationism

Questions 4-7.

DIRECTIONS: Questions 4 through 7 are to be answered SOLELY on the basis of the following passage.

    Data processing is by no means a new invention. In one form or another, it has been carried on throughout the entire history of civilization. In its most general sense, data processing means organizing data so that it can be used for a specific purpose-a procedure commonly known simply as *record-keeping* or *paperwork*. With the development of modern office equipment, and particularly with the recent introduction of computers, the techniques of data processing have become highly elaborate and sophisticated, but the basic purpose remains the same: Turning raw data into useful information.

    The key concept here is usefulness. The data, or input, that is to be processed can be compared to the raw material that is to go into a manufacturing process. The information, or output, that results from data processing—like the finished product of a manufacturer—should be clearly usable. A collection of data has little value unless it is converted into information that serves a specific function.

4. The expression *paperwork*, as it is used in this passage,

   A. shows that the author regards such operations as a waste of time
   B. has the same general meaning as *data processing*
   C. refers to methods of record-keeping that are no longer in use
   D. indicates that the public does not understand the purpose of data processing

5. The above passage indicates that the use of computers has

   A. greatly simplified the clerical work in an office
   B. led to more complicated systems for the handling of data
   C. had no effect whatsoever on data processing
   D. made other modern office machines obsolete

6. Which of the following BEST expresses the basic principle of data processing as it is described in the above passage?

   A. Input-processing-output
   B. Historical record-keeping-modern techniques -specific functions
   C. Office equipment-computer-accurate data
   D. Raw material-manufacturer-retailer

7. According to the above passage, data processing may be described as

   A. a new management technique
   B. computer technology
   C. information output
   D. record-keeping

Questions 8-10.

DIRECTIONS: Questions 8 through 10 are to be answered SOLELY on the basis of the following passage.

    A loan receipt is an instrument devised to permit the insurance company to bring an action against the wrongdoer in the name of the insured despite the fact that the insured no longer has any financial interest in the outcome. It provides, in effect, that the amount of the loss is advanced to the insured as a loan which is repayable only up to the extent of any recovery made from the wrongdoer. The insured further agrees to enter and prosecute suit against the wrongdoer in his own name. Such a receipt substitutes a loan for a payment for the purpose of permitting the insurance company to press its action against the wrongdoer in the name of the insured.

8. According to the above passage, the purpose behind the use of a loan receipt is to 8.____

    A. guarantee that the insurance company gets repayment from the person insured
    B. insure repayment of all expenditures to the named insured
    C. make it possible for the insurance company to sue in the name of the policyowner
    D. prevent the wrongdoer from escaping the natural consequences of his act

9. According to the above passage, the amount of the loan which must be paid back to the insurance company equals but does NOT exceed the amount 9.____

    A. of the loss
    B. on the face of the policy
    C. paid to the insured
    D. recovered from the wrongdoer

10. According to the above passage, by giving a loan receipt, the person insured agrees to 10.____

    A. a suit against the wrongdoer in his own name
    B. forego any financial gain from the outcome of the suit
    C. institute an action on behalf of the insurance company
    D. repay the insurance company for the loan received

Questions 11-12.

DIRECTIONS: Questions 11 and 12 are to be answered SOLELY on the basis of the following passage.

    Open air markets originally came into existence spontaneously when groups of pushcart peddlers congregated in spots where business was good. Good business induced them to return to these spots daily and, thus, unofficial open air markets arose. These peddlers paid no fees, and the city received no revenue from them. Confusion and disorder reigned in these unsupervised markets; the earliest arrivals secured the best locations, unless or until forcibly ejected by stronger or tougher peddlers. Although the open air markets supplied a definite need in the community, there were many detrimental factors involved in their operation. They were unsightly, created unsanitary conditions in market streets by the deposit of garbage and waste and were a definite obstruction to traffic, as well as a fire hazard.

11. On the basis of the above passage, the MOST accurate of the following statements is:

    A. Each peddler in the original open air markets had his own fixed location.
    B. Open air markets were originally organized by means of agreements between groups of pushcart peddlers.
    C. The locations of these markets depended upon the amount of business the vendors were able to do.
    D. There was confusion and disorder in these open air markets because the peddlers were not required to pay any fees to the city.

12. Of the following, the MOST valid implication which can be made on the basis of the above passage is that the

    A. detrimental aspect of the operations of open air markets was the probable reason for the creation of enclosed markets under the supervision of the Department of Markets
    B. open air markets could not supply any community need without proper supervision
    C. original open air markets were good examples of the operation of fair competition in business
    D. possibility of obtaining a source of revenue was probably the most important reason for the city's ultimate undertaking of the supervision of open air markets

Questions 13-14.

DIRECTIONS: Questions 13 and 14 are to be answered SOLELY on the basis of the following passage.

A person who displays on his window, door, or in his place of business words or letters in Hebraic characters other than the word *kosher,* or any sign, emblem, insignia, six-pointed star, symbol or mark in simulation of same, without displaying in conjunction there-with in English letters of at least the same size as such characters, signs, emblems, insignia or marks, the words *we sell kosher meat and food only* or *we sell non-kosher meat and food only* or *we sell both kosher and non-kosher meat and food,* as the case may be, is guilty of a misdemeanor. Possession of non-kosher meat and food in any place of business advertising the sale of kosher meat and food only is presumptive evidence that the person in possession exposes the same for sale with intent to defraud, in violation of the provisions of this section.

13. Of the following, the MOST valid implication that can be made on the basis of the above passage is that a person who

    A. displays on his window a six-pointed star in addition to the word *kosher* in Hebraic letters is guilty of intent to defraud
    B. displays on his window the word *kosher* in Hebraic characters intends to indicate that he has only kosher food for sale
    C. sells both kosher and non-kosher food in the same place of business is guilty of a misdemeanor
    D. sells only that type of food which can be characterized as neither kosher nor non-kosher, such as fruit and vegetables, without an explanatory sign in English is guilty of intent to defraud

14. Of the following, the one which would constitute a violation of the rules of the above passage is a case in which a person

   A. displays the word *kosher* on his window in Hebraic letters has only kosher meat and food in the store but has some non-kosher meat in the rear of the establishment
   B. selling both kosher and non-kosher meat and food uses words in Hebraic letters, other than the word *kosher*, on his window and a sign of the same size letters in English stating *we sell both kosher and non-kosher meat and food*
   C. selling only kosher meat and food uses words in Hebraic letters, other than the word *kosher*, on his window and a sign of the same size letters in English stating *we sell kosher meat and food only*
   D. selling only non-kosher meat and food displays a six-pointed star on his window and a sign of the same size letters in English stating *we sell only non-kosher meat and food*

Questions 15-16.

DIRECTIONS: Questions 15 and 16 are to be answered SOLELY on the basis of the following passage.

COMMODITIES IN GLASS BOTTLES OR JARS

The contents of the bottle may be stated in terms of weight or of fluid measure, the weight being indicated in terms of pounds and ounces and the fluid measure being indicated in terms of gallons, quarts, pints, half-pints, gills, or fluid ounces. When contents are liquid, the amount should not be stated in terms of weight. The marking indicating content is to be on a tag attached to the bottle or upon a label. The letters shall be in bold-faced type at least one-ninth of an inch (1/9") in height for bottles or jars having a capacity of a gill, half-pint, pint, or multiples of a pint, and letters at least three-sixteenths of an inch (3/16") in height for bottles of other capacities, on a part of the tag or label free from other printing or ornamentation, leaving a clear space around the marking which indicates the contents.

15. Of the following, the one which does NOT meet the requirements of the above passage is a

   A. bottle of cooking oil with a label stating *contents—16 fluid ounces* in appropriate sized letters
   B. bottle of vinegar with a label stating *contents—8 ounces avoir.* in appropriate sized letters
   C. glass jar filled with instant coffee with a label stating *contents—1 lb. 3 ozs. avoir.* in appropriate sized letters
   D. glass jar filled with liquid bleach with a label stating *contents—1 quart* in appropriate sized letters

16. Of the following, the one which does meet the requirements of the above passage is a

   A. bottle filled with a low-calorie liquid sweetener with a label stating *contents—3 fluid ounces* in letters 1/12" high
   B. bottle filled with ammonia solution for cleaning with a label stating *contents—1 pint* in letters 1/10" high

C. jar filled with baking powder with a label stating *contents—$\frac{1}{2}$ pint* in letters $\frac{1}{4}$" high

D. jar filled with hard candy with a label stating *contents—1 lb. avoir.* in letters $\frac{1}{2}$" high

Question 17.

DIRECTIONS: Question 17 is to be answered SOLELY on the basis of the information contained in the following passage.

DEALERS IN SECOND HAND DEVICES

1. It shall be unlawful for any person to engage in or conduct the business of dealing in, trading in, selling, receiving, or repairing condemned, rebuilt, or used weighing or measuring devices without a permit therefor.

2. Such permit shall expire on the twenty-eighth day of February next succeeding the date of issuance thereof.

3. Every person engaged in the above business, within five days after the making of a repair, or the sale and delivery of a repaired, rebuilt, or used weighing or measuring device, shall serve notice in writing on the commissioner giving the name and address of the person for whom the repair has been made or to whom a repaired, rebuilt, or used weighing or measuring device has been sold or delivered, and shall include a statement that such device has been so altered, repaired, or rebuilt as to conform to the regulations of the department.

17. According to the above passage, the MOST accurate of the following statements is: 17.___

A. A permit issued to engage in the business mentioned above, first issued on April 23, 1968, expired on February 28, 1969.
B. A rebuilt or repaired weighing or measuring device should not operate with less error than the tolerances permitted by the regulations of the department.
C. If a used scale in good condition is sold, it is not necessary for the seller to notify the commissioner of the name and address of the buyer.
D. There is a difference in the time required to notify the commissioner of a repair or of a sale of a repaired device.

Questions 18-19.

DIRECTIONS: Questions 18 and 19 are to be answered SOLELY on the basis of the following passage.

A. It shall be unlawful for any person, firm, or corporation to sell or offer for sale at retail for use in internal combustion engines in motor vehicles any gasoline unless such seller shall post and keep continuously posted on the individual pump or other dispensing device from which such gasoline is sold or offered for sale a sign or placard not less than seven inches in height and eight inches in width nor larger than twelve inches in height and twelve inches in width and stating clearly in numbers of uniform size the selling price or prices per gallon of such gasoline so sold or offered for sale from such pump or other dispensing device.

B. The amount of governmental tax to be collected in connection with the sale of such gasoline shall be stated on such sign or placard and separately and apart from such selling price or prices.

18. The one of the following price signs posted on a gasoline pump which would be in violation of the above passage is a sign _____ square inches in size and _____ inches high.

   A. 144; 12   B. 84; 7   C. 72; 12   D. 60; 8

19. According to the above passage, the LEAST accurate of the following statements is:

   A. Gasoline may be sold from a dispensing device other than a pump.
   B. If two different pumps are used to sell the same grade of gasoline, a price sign must appear on each pump.
   C. The amount of governmental tax and the price of the gasoline must not be stated on the same sign.
   D. The sizes of the numbers used on a sign to indicate the price of gasoline must be the same.

Questions 20-21.

DIRECTIONS: Questions 20 and 21 are to be answered SOLELY on the basis of the following passage.

In all systems of weights and measures based on one or more arbitrary fundamental units, the concrete representation of the unit in the form of a standard is necessary, and the construction and preservation of such a standard is a matter of primary importance. Therefore, it is essential that the standard should be so constructed as to be as nearly permanent and invariable as human ingenuity can contrive. The reference of all measures to an original standard is essential for their correctness, and such a standard must be maintained and preserved in its integrity by some responsible authority which is thus able to provide against the use of false weights and measures. Accordingly, from earliest times, standards were constructed and preserved under the direction of kings and priests, and the temples were a favorite place for their deposit. Later, this duty was assumed by the government, and today we find the integrity of standards of weights and measures safeguarded by international agreement.

20. Of the following, the MOST valid implication which can be made on the basis of the above passage is that

   A. fundamental units of systems of weights and measures should be represented by quantities so constructed that they are specific and constant
   B. in the earliest times, standards were so constructed that they were as permanent and invariable as modern ones
   C. international agreement has practically relieved the U.S. government of the necessity of preserving standards of weights and measures
   D. the preservation of standards is of less importance than the ingenuity used in their construction

21. Of the following, the MOST appropriate title for the above passage is

	A. THE CONSTRUCTION AND PRESERVATION OF STANDARDS OF WEIGHTS AND MEASURES
	B. THE FIXING OF RESPONSIBILITY FOR THE ESTABLISHMENT OF STANDARDS OF WEIGHTS AND MEASURES
	C. THE HISTORY OF SYSTEMS OF WEIGHTS AND MEASURES
	D. THE VALUE OF PROPER STANDARDS IN PROVIDING CORRECT WEIGHTS AND MEASURES

Questions 22-23.

DIRECTIONS: Questions 22 and 23 are to be answered SOLELY on the basis of the following passage.

Accurate weighing and good scales insure that excess is not given just for the sake of good measure. No more striking example of the fundamental importance of correct weighing to the business man is found than in the simple and usual relation where a charge or value is obtained by multiplying a weight by a unit price. For example, a scale may weigh *light,* that is, the actual quantity delivered is in excess by 1 percent. The actual result is that the seller taxes himself. If his profit is supposed to be 10 percent of total sales, an overweight of 1 percent represents 10 percent of that profit. Under these conditions, the situation is as though the seller were required to pay a sales tax equivalent to what he is taxing himself.

22. Of the following, the MOST valid implication which can be made on the basis of the above passage is that

	A. consistent use of scales that weigh *light* will reduce sellers' profits
	B. no good businessman would give any buyer more than the weight required even if his scale is accurate
	C. the kind of situation described in the above passage could not arise if sales were being made of merchandise sold by the yard
	D. the use of incorrect scales is one of the reasons causing governments to impose sales taxes

23. According to the above passage, the MOST accurate of the following statements is:

	A. If his scale weighs *light* by an amount of 2 percent, the seller would deliver only 98 pounds when 100 pounds was the amount agreed upon.
	B. If the seller's scale weighs *heavy,* the buyer will receive an amount in excess of what he intended to purchase.
	C. If the seller's scale weighs *light* by an amount of 1 percent, a buyer who agreed to purchase 50 pounds of merchandise would actually receive 50 $\frac{1}{2}$ pounds.
	D. The use of a scale which delivers an amount which is in excess of that required is an example of deliberate fraud.

Questions 24-25.

DIRECTIONS: Questions 24 and 25 are to be answered SOLELY on the basis of the following passage.

Food shall be deemed to be misbranded:
1. If its labeling is false or misleading in any particular.

2. If any word, statement, or other information required by or under authority of this article to appear on the label or labeling is not prominently placed thereon with such conspicuousness (as compared with other words, statements, designs, or devices in the labeling) and in such terms as to render it likely to be read and understood by the ordinary individual under customary conditions of purchase and use.

3. If it purports to be or is represented as a food for which a standard of quality has been prescribed and its quality falls below such standard, unless its label bears a statement that it falls below such standard.

24. According to the above passage, the MOST accurate of the following statements is:

    A. A food may be considered misbranded if the label contains a considerable amount of information which is not required.
    B. If a consumer purchased one type of canned food, although he intended to buy another, the food is probably misbranded.
    C. If a food is used in large amounts by a group of people of certain foreign origin, it can be considered misbranded unless the label is in the foreign language with which they are familiar.
    D. The required information on a label is likely to be in larger print than other information which may appear on it.

25. According to the above passage, the one of the following foods which may be considered to be misbranded is a

    A. can of peaches with a label which carries the brand name of the packer but states *Below Standard in Quality*
    B. can of vegetables with a label on which is printed a shield which states *U.S. Grade B*
    C. package of frozen food which has some pertinent information printed on it in very small type which a customer cannot read and which the store manager cannot read when asked to do so by the customer
    D. package of margarine of the same size as the usual package of butter, kept near the butter, but clearly labeled as margarine

KEY (CORRECT ANSWERS)

1. C
2. D
3. B
4. B
5. B

6. A
7. D
8. C
9. D
10. A

11. C
12. A
13. B
14. A
15. B

16. D
17. A
18. C
19. C
20. A

21. D
22. A
23. C
24. D
25. C

GLOSSARY OF LEGAL TERMS

TABLE OF CONTENTS

	Page
Action ... Affiant	1
Affidavit ... At Bar	2
At Issue ... Burden of Proof	3
Business ... Commute	4
Complainant ... Conviction	5
Cooperative ... Demur (v.)	6
Demurrage ... Endorsement	7
Enjoin ... Facsimile	8
Factor ... Guilty	9
Habeas Corpus ... Incumbrance	10
Indemnify ... Laches	11
Landlord and Tenant ... Malice	12
Mandamus ... Obiter Dictum	13
Object (v.) ... Perjury	14
Perpetuity ... Proclamation	15
Proffered Evidence ... Referee	16
Referendum ... Stare Decisis	17
State ... Term	18
Testamentary ... Warrant (Warranty) (v.)	19
Warrant (n.) ... Zoning	20

GLOSSARY OF LEGAL TERMS

A

ACTION - "Action" includes a civil action and a criminal action.

A FORTIORI - A term meaning you can reason one thing from the existence of certain facts.

A POSTERIORI - From what goes after; from effect to cause.

A PRIORI - From what goes before; from cause to effect.

AB INITIO - From the beginning.

ABATE - To diminish or put an end to.

ABET - To encourage the commission of a crime.

ABEYANCE - Suspension, temporary suppression.

ABIDE - To accept the consequences of.

ABJURE - To renounce; give up.

ABRIDGE - To reduce; contract; diminish.

ABROGATE - To annul, repeal, or destroy.

ABSCOND - To hide or absent oneself to avoid legal action.

ABSTRACT - A summary.

ABUT - To border on, to touch.

ACCESS - Approach; in real property law it means the right of the owner of property to the use of the highway or road next to his land, without obstruction by intervening property owners.

ACCESSORY - In criminal law, it means the person who contributes or aids in the commission of a crime.

ACCOMMODATED PARTY - One to whom credit is extended on the strength of another person signing a commercial paper.

ACCOMMODATION PAPER - A commercial paper to which the accommodating party has put his name.

ACCOMPLICE - In criminal law, it means a person who together with the principal offender commits a crime.

ACCORD - An agreement to accept something different or less than that to which one is entitled, which extinguishes the entire obligation.

ACCOUNT - A statement of mutual demands in the nature of debt and credit between parties.

ACCRETION - The act of adding to a thing; in real property law, it means gradual accumulation of land by natural causes.

ACCRUE - To grow to; to be added to.

ACKNOWLEDGMENT - The act of going before an official authorized to take acknowledgments, and acknowledging an act as one's own.

ACQUIESCENCE - A silent appearance of consent.

ACQUIT - To legally determine the innocence of one charged with a crime.

AD INFINITUM - Indefinitely.

AD LITEM - For the suit.

AD VALOREM - According to value.

ADJECTIVE LAW - Rules of procedure.

ADJUDICATION - The judgment given in a case.

ADMIRALTY - Court having jurisdiction over maritime cases.

ADULT - Sixteen years old or over (in criminal law).

ADVANCE - In commercial law, it means to pay money or render other value before it is due.

ADVERSE - Opposed; contrary.

ADVOCATE - (v.) To speak in favor of;
(n.) One who assists, defends, or pleads for another.

AFFIANT - A person who makes and signs an affidavit.

AFFIDAVIT - A written and sworn to declaration of facts, voluntarily made.

AFFINITY - The relationship between persons through marriage with the kindred of each other; distinguished from consanguinity, which is the relationship by blood.

AFFIRM - To ratify; also when an appellate court affirms a judgment, decree, or order, it means that it is valid and right and must stand as rendered in the lower court.

AFOREMENTIONED; AFORESAID - Before or already said.

AGENT - One who represents and acts for another.

AID AND COMFORT - To help; encourage.

ALIAS - A name not one's true name.

ALIBI - A claim of not being present at a certain place at a certain time.

ALLEGE - To assert.

ALLOTMENT - A share or portion.

AMBIGUITY - Uncertainty; capable of being understood in more than one way.

AMENDMENT - Any language made or proposed as a change in some principal writing.

AMICUS CURIAE - A friend of the court; one who has an interest in a case, although not a party in the case, who volunteers advice upon matters of law to the judge. For example, a brief amicus curiae.

AMORTIZATION - To provide for a gradual extinction of (a future obligation) in advance of maturity, especially, by periodical contributions to a sinking fund which will be adequate to discharge a debt or make a replacement when it becomes necessary.

ANCILLARY - Aiding, auxiliary.

ANNOTATION - A note added by way of comment or explanation.

ANSWER - A written statement made by a defendant setting forth the grounds of his defense.

ANTE - Before.

ANTE MORTEM - Before death.

APPEAL - The removal of a case from a lower court to one of superior jurisdiction for the purpose of obtaining a review.

APPEARANCE - Coming into court as a party to a suit.

APPELLANT - The party who takes an appeal from one court or jurisdiction to another (appellate) court for review.

APPELLEE - The party against whom an appeal is taken.

APPROPRIATE - To make a thing one's own.

APPROPRIATION - Prescribing the destination of a thing; the act of the legislature designating a particular fund, to be applied to some object of government expenditure.

APPURTENANT - Belonging to; accessory or incident to.

ARBITER - One who decides a dispute; a referee.

ARBITRARY - Unreasoned; not governed by any fixed rules or standard.

ARGUENDO - By way of argument.

ARRAIGN - To call the prisoner before the court to answer to a charge.

ASSENT - A declaration of willingness to do something in compliance with a request.

ASSERT - Declare.

ASSESS - To fix the rate or amount.

ASSIGN - To transfer; to appoint; to select for a particular purpose.

ASSIGNEE - One who receives an assignment.

ASSIGNOR - One who makes an assignment.

AT BAR - Before the court.

AT ISSUE - When parties in an action come to a point where one asserts something and the other denies it.
ATTACH - Seize property by court order and sometimes arrest a person.
ATTEST - To witness a will, etc.; act of attestation.
AVERMENT - A positive statement of facts.

B

BAIL - To obtain the release of a person from legal custody by giving security and promising that he shall appear in court; to deliver (goods, etc.) in trust to a person for a special purpose.
BAILEE - One to whom personal property is delivered under a contract of bailment.
BAILMENT - Delivery of personal property to another to be held for a certain purpose and to be returned when the purpose is accomplished.
BAILOR - The party who delivers goods to another, under a contract of bailment.
BANC (OR BANK) - Bench; the place where a court sits permanently or regularly; also the assembly of all the judges of a court.
BANKRUPT - An insolvent person, technically, one declared to be bankrupt after a bankruptcy proceeding.
BAR - The legal profession.
BARRATRY - Exciting groundless judicial proceedings.
BARTER - A contract by which parties exchange goods for other goods.
BATTERY - Illegal interfering with another's person.
BEARER - In commercial law, it means the person in possession of a commercial paper which is payable to the bearer.
BENCH - The court itself or the judge.
BENEFICIARY - A person benefiting under a will, trust, or agreement.
BEST EVIDENCE RULE, THE - Except as otherwise provided by statute, no evidence other than the writing itself is admissible to prove the content of a writing. This section shall be known and may be cited as the best evidence rule.
BEQUEST - A gift of personal property under a will.
BILL - A formal written statement of complaint to a court of justice; also, a draft of an act of the legislature before it becomes a law; also, accounts for goods sold, services rendered, or work done.
BONA FIDE - In or with good faith; honestly.
BOND - An instrument by which the maker promises to pay a sum of money to another, usually providing that upon performances of a certain condition the obligation shall be void.
BOYCOTT - A plan to prevent the carrying on of a business by wrongful means.
BREACH - The breaking or violating of a law, or the failure to carry out a duty.
BRIEF - A written document, prepared by a lawyer to serve as the basis of an argument upon a case in court, usually an appellate court.
BURDEN OF PRODUCING EVIDENCE - The obligation of a party to introduce evidence sufficient to avoid a ruling against him on the issue.
BURDEN OF PROOF - The obligation of a party to establish by evidence a requisite degree of belief concerning a fact in the mind of the trier of fact or the court. The burden of proof may require a party to raise a reasonable doubt concerning the existence of nonexistence of a fact or that he establish the existence or nonexistence of a fact by a preponderance of the evidence, by clear and convincing proof, or by proof beyond a reasonable doubt.

    Except as otherwise provided by law, the burden of proof requires proof by a preponderance of the evidence.

BUSINESS, A - Shall include every kind of business, profession, occupation, calling or operation of institutions, whether carried on for profit or not.

BY-LAWS - Regulations, ordinances, or rules enacted by a corporation, association, etc., for its own government.

C

CANON - A doctrine; also, a law or rule, of a church or association in particular.

CAPIAS - An order to arrest.

CAPTION - In a pleading, deposition or other paper connected with a case in court, it is the heading or introductory clause which shows the names of the parties, name of the court, number of the case on the docket or calendar, etc.

CARRIER - A person or corporation undertaking to transport persons or property.

CASE - A general term for an action, cause, suit, or controversy before a judicial body.

CAUSE - A suit, litigation or action before a court.

CAVEAT EMPTOR - Let the buyer beware. This term expresses the rule that the purchaser of an article must examine, judge, and test it for himself, being bound to discover any obvious defects or imperfections.

CERTIFICATE - A written representation that some legal formality has been complied with.

CERTIORARI - To be informed of; the name of a writ issued by a superior court directing the lower court to send up to the former the record and proceedings of a case.

CHANGE OF VENUE - To remove place of trial from one place to another.

CHARGE - An obligation or duty; a formal complaint; an instruction of the court to the jury upon a case.

CHARTER - (n.) The authority by virtue of which an organized body acts;
       (v.) in mercantile law, it means to hire or lease a vehicle or vessel for transportation.

CHATTEL - An article of personal property.

CHATTEL MORTGAGE - A mortgage on personal property.

CIRCUIT - A division of the country, for the administration of justice; a geographical area served by a court.

CITATION - The act of the court by which a person is summoned or cited; also, a reference to legal authority.

CIVIL (ACTIONS)- It indicates the private rights and remedies of individuals in contrast to the word "criminal" (actions) which relates to prosecution for violation of laws.

CLAIM (n.) - Any demand held or asserted as of right.

CODICIL - An addition to a will.

CODIFY - To arrange the laws of a country into a code.

COGNIZANCE - Notice or knowledge.

COLLATERAL - By the side; accompanying; an article or thing given to secure performance of a promise.

COMITY - Courtesy; the practice by which one court follows the decision of another court on the same question.

COMMIT - To perform, as an act; to perpetrate, as a crime; to send a person to prison.

COMMON LAW - As distinguished from law created by the enactment of the legislature (called statutory law), it relates to those principles and rules of action which derive their authority solely from usages and customs of immemorial antiquity, particularly with reference to the ancient unwritten law of England. The written pronouncements of the common law are found in court decisions.

COMMUTE - Change punishment to one less severe.

COMPLAINANT - One who applies to the court for legal redress.
COMPLAINT - The pleading of a plaintiff in a civil action; or a charge that a person has committed a specified offense.
COMPROMISE - An arrangement for settling a dispute by agreement.
CONCUR - To agree, consent.
CONCURRENT - Running together, at the same time.
CONDEMNATION - Taking private property for public use on payment therefor.
CONDITION - Mode or state of being; a qualification or restriction.
CONDUCT - Active and passive behavior; both verbal and nonverbal.
CONFESSION - Voluntary statement of guilt of crime.
CONFIDENTIAL COMMUNICATION BETWEEN CLIENT AND LAWYER - Information transmitted between a client and his lawyer in the course of that relationship and in confidence by a means which, so far as the client is aware, discloses the information to no third persons other than those who are present to further the interest of the client in the consultation or those to whom disclosure is reasonably necessary for the transmission of the information or the accomplishment of the purpose for which the lawyer is consulted, and includes a legal opinion formed and the advice given by the lawyer in the course of that relationship.
CONFRONTATION - Witness testifying in presence of defendant.
CONSANGUINITY - Blood relationship.
CONSIGN - To give in charge; commit; entrust; to send or transmit goods to a merchant, factor, or agent for sale.
CONSIGNEE - One to whom a consignment is made.
CONSIGNOR - One who sends or makes a consignment.
CONSPIRACY - In criminal law, it means an agreement between two or more persons to commit an unlawful act.
CONSPIRATORS - Persons involved in a conspiracy.
CONSTITUTION - The fundamental law of a nation or state.
CONSTRUCTION OF GENDERS - The masculine gender includes the feminine and neuter.
CONSTRUCTION OF SINGULAR AND PLURAL - The singular number includes the plural; and the plural, the singular.
CONSTRUCTION OF TENSES - The present tense includes the past and future tenses; and the future, the present.
CONSTRUCTIVE - An act or condition assumed from other parts or conditions.
CONSTRUE - To ascertain the meaning of language.
CONSUMMATE - To complete.
CONTIGUOUS - Adjoining; touching; bounded by.
CONTINGENT - Possible, but not assured; dependent upon some condition.
CONTINUANCE - The adjournment or postponement of an action pending in a court.
CONTRA - Against, opposed to; contrary.
CONTRACT - An agreement between two or more persons to do or not to do a particular thing.
CONTROVERT - To dispute, deny.
CONVERSION - Dealing with the personal property of another as if it were one's own, without right.
CONVEYANCE - An instrument transferring title to land.
CONVICTION - Generally, the result of a criminal trial which ends in a judgment or sentence that the defendant is guilty as charged.

COOPERATIVE - A cooperative is a voluntary organization of persons with a common interest, formed and operated along democratic lines for the purpose of supplying services at cost to its members and other patrons, who contribute both capital and business.
CORPUS DELICTI - The body of a crime; the crime itself.
CORROBORATE - To strengthen; to add weight by additional evidence.
COUNTERCLAIM - A claim presented by a defendant in opposition to or deduction from the claim of the plaintiff.
COUNTY - Political subdivision of a state.
COVENANT - Agreement.
CREDIBLE - Worthy of belief.
CREDITOR - A person to whom a debt is owing by another person, called the "debtor."
CRIMINAL ACTION - Includes criminal proceedings.
CRIMINAL INFORMATION - Same as complaint.
CRITERION (sing.)
CRITERIA (plural) - A means or tests for judging; a standard or standards.
CROSS-EXAMINATION - Examination of a witness by a party other than the direct examiner upon a matter that is within the scope of the direct examination of the witness.
CULPABLE - Blamable.
CY-PRES - As near as (possible). The rule of *cy-pres* is a rule for the construction of instruments in equity by which the intention of the party is carried out *as near as may be*, when it would be impossible or illegal to give it literal effect.

D

DAMAGES - A monetary compensation, which may be recovered in the courts by any person who has suffered loss, or injury, whether to his person, property or rights through the unlawful act or omission or negligence of another.
DECLARANT - A person who makes a statement.
DE FACTO - In fact; actually but without legal authority.
DE JURE - Of right; legitimate; lawful.
DE MINIMIS - Very small or trifling.
DE NOVO - Anew; afresh; a second time.
DEBT - A specified sum of money owing to one person from another, including not only the obligation of the debtor to pay, but the right of the creditor to receive and enforce payment.
DECEDENT - A dead person.
DECISION - A judgment or decree pronounced by a court in determination of a case.
DECREE - An order of the court, determining the rights of all parties to a suit.
DEED - A writing containing a contract sealed and delivered; particularly to convey real property.
DEFALCATION - Misappropriation of funds.
DEFAMATION - Injuring one's reputation by false statements.
DEFAULT - The failure to fulfill a duty, observe a promise, discharge an obligation, or perform an agreement.
DEFENDANT - The person defending or denying; the party against whom relief or recovery is sought in an action or suit.
DEFRAUD - To practice fraud; to cheat or trick.
DELEGATE (v.)- To entrust to the care or management of another.
DELICTUS - A crime.
DEMUR (v.) - To dispute the sufficiency in law of the pleading of the other side.

DEMURRAGE - In maritime law, it means, the sum fixed or allowed as remuneration to the owners of a ship for the detention of their vessel beyond the number of days allowed for loading and unloading or for sailing; also used in railroad terminology.
DENIAL - A form of pleading; refusing to admit the truth of a statement, charge, etc.
DEPONENT - One who gives testimony under oath reduced to writing.
DEPOSITION - Testimony given under oath outside of court for use in court or for the purpose of obtaining information in preparation for trial of a case.
DETERIORATION - A degeneration such as from decay, corrosion or disintegration.
DETRIMENT - Any loss or harm to person or property.
DEVIATION - A turning aside.
DEVISE - A gift of real property by the last will and testament of the donor.
DICTUM (sing.)
DICTA (plural) - Any statements made by the court in an opinion concerning some rule of law not necessarily involved nor essential to the determination of the case.
DIRECT EVIDENCE - Evidence that directly proves a fact, without an inference or presumption, and which in itself if true, conclusively establishes that fact.
DIRECT EXAMINATION - The first examination of a witness upon a matter that is not within the scope of a previous examination of the witness.
DISAFFIRM - To repudiate.
DISMISS - In an action or suit, it means to dispose of the case without any further consideration or hearing.
DISSENT - To denote disagreement of one or more judges of a court with the decision passed by the majority upon a case before them.
DOCKET (n.) - A formal record, entered in brief, of the proceedings in a court.
DOCTRINE - A rule, principle, theory of law.
DOMICILE - That place where a man has his true, fixed and permanent home to which whenever he is absent he has the intention of returning.
DRAFT (n.) - A commercial paper ordering payment of money drawn by one person on another.
DRAWEE - The person who is requested to pay the money.
DRAWER - The person who draws the commercial paper and addresses it to the drawee.
DUPLICATE - A counterpart produced by the same impression as the original enlargements and miniatures, or by mechanical or electronic re-recording, or by chemical reproduction, or by other equivalent technique which accurately reproduces the original.
DURESS - Use of force to compel performance or non-performance of an act.

E

EASEMENT - A liberty, privilege, or advantage without profit, in the lands of another.
EGRESS - Act or right of going out or leaving; emergence.
EIUSDEM GENERIS - Of the same kind, class or nature. A rule used in the construction of language in a legal document.
EMBEZZLEMENT - To steal; to appropriate fraudulently to one's own use property entrusted to one's care.
EMBRACERY - Unlawful attempt to influence jurors, etc., but not by offering value.
EMINENT DOMAIN - The right of a state to take private property for public use.
ENACT - To make into a law.
ENDORSEMENT - Act of writing one's name on the back of a note, bill or similar written instrument.

ENJOIN - To require a person, by writ of injunction from a court of equity, to perform or to abstain or desist from some act.
ENTIRETY - The whole; that which the law considers as one whole, and not capable of being divided into parts.
ENTRAPMENT - Inducing one to commit a crime so as to arrest him.
ENUMERATED - Mentioned specifically; designated.
ENURE - To operate or take effect.
EQUITY - In its broadest sense, this term denotes the spirit and the habit of fairness, justness, and right dealing which regulate the conduct of men.
ERROR - A mistake of law, or the false or irregular application of law as will nullify the judicial proceedings.
ESCROW - A deed, bond or other written engagement, delivered to a third person, to be delivered by him only upon the performance or fulfillment of some condition.
ESTATE - The interest which any one has in lands, or in any other subject of property.
ESTOP - To stop, bar, or impede.
ESTOPPEL - A rule of law which prevents a man from alleging or denying a fact, because of his own previous act.
ET AL. (alii) - And others.
ET SEQ. (sequential) - And the following.
ET UX. (uxor) - And wife.
EVIDENCE - Testimony, writings, material objects, or other things presented to the senses that are offered to prove the existence or non-existence of a fact.
    Means from which inferences may be drawn as a basis of proof in duly constituted judicial or fact finding tribunals, and includes testimony in the form of opinion and hearsay.
EX CONTRACTU
EX DELICTO - In law, rights and causes of action are divided into two classes, those arising *ex contractu* (from a contract) and those arising *ex delicto* (from a delict or tort).
EX OFFICIO - From office; by virtue of the office.
EX PARTE - On one side only; by or for one.
EX POST FACTO - After the fact.
EX POST FACTO LAW - A law passed after an act was done which retroactively makes such act a crime.
EX REL. (relations) - Upon relation or information.
EXCEPTION - An objection upon a matter of law to a decision made, either before or after judgment by a court.
EXECUTOR (male)
EXECUTRIX (female) - A person who has been appointed by will to execute the will.
EXECUTORY - That which is yet to be executed or performed.
EXEMPT - To release from some liability to which others are subject.
EXONERATION - The removal of a burden, charge or duty.
EXTRADITION - Surrender of a fugitive from one nation to another.

F

F.A.S.- "Free alongside ship"; delivery at dock for ship named.
F.O.B.- "Free on board"; seller will deliver to car, truck, vessel, or other conveyance by which goods are to be transported, without expense or risk of loss to the buyer or consignee.
FABRICATE - To construct; to invent a false story.
FACSIMILE - An exact or accurate copy of an original instrument.

FACTOR - A commercial agent.
FEASANCE - The doing of an act.
FELONIOUS - Criminal, malicious.
FELONY - Generally, a criminal offense that may be punished by death or imprisonment for more than one year as differentiated from a misdemeanor.
FEME SOLE - A single woman.
FIDUCIARY - A person who is invested with rights and powers to be exercised for the benefit of another person.
FIERI FACIAS - A writ of execution commanding the sheriff to levy and collect the amount of a judgment from the goods and chattels of the judgment debtor.
FINDING OF FACT - Determination from proof or judicial notice of the existence of a fact. A ruling implies a supporting finding of fact; no separate or formal finding is required unless required by a statute of this state.
FISCAL - Relating to accounts or the management of revenue.
FORECLOSURE (sale) - A sale of mortgaged property to obtain satisfaction of the mortgage out of the sale proceeds.
FORFEITURE - A penalty, a fine.
FORGERY - Fabricating or producing falsely, counterfeited.
FORTUITOUS - Accidental.
FORUM - A court of justice; a place of jurisdiction.
FRAUD - Deception; trickery.
FREEHOLDER - One who owns real property.
FUNGIBLE - Of such kind or nature that one specimen or part may be used in the place of another.

G

GARNISHEE - Person garnished.
GARNISHMENT - A legal process to reach the money or effects of a defendant, in the possession or control of a third person.
GRAND JURY - Not less than 16, not more than 23 citizens of a county sworn to inquire into crimes committed or triable in the county.
GRANT - To agree to; convey, especially real property.
GRANTEE - The person to whom a grant is made.
GRANTOR - The person by whom a grant is made.
GRATUITOUS - Given without a return, compensation or consideration.
GRAVAMEN - The grievance complained of or the substantial cause of a criminal action.
GUARANTY (n.) - A promise to answer for the payment of some debt, or the performance of some duty, in case of the failure of another person, who, in the first instance, is liable for such payment or performance.
GUARDIAN - The person, committee, or other representative authorized by law to protect the person or estate or both of an incompetent (or of a *sui juris* person having a guardian) and to act for him in matters affecting his person or property or both. An incompetent is a person under disability imposed by law.
GUILTY - Establishment of the fact that one has committed a breach of conduct; especially, a violation of law.

H

HABEAS CORPUS - You have the body; the name given to a variety of writs, having for their object to bring a party before a court or judge for decision as to whether such person is being lawfully held prisoner.
HABENDUM - In conveyancing; it is the clause in a deed conveying land which defines the extent of ownership to be held by the grantee.
HEARING - A proceeding whereby the arguments of the interested parties are heared.
HEARSAY - A type of testimony given by a witness who relates, not what he knows personally, but what others have told hi, or what he has heard said by others.
HEARSAY RULE, THE - (a) "Hearsay evidence" is evidence of a statement that was made other than by a witness while testifying at the hearing and that is offered to prove the truth of the matter stated; (b) Except as provided by law, hearsay evidence is inadmissible; (c) This section shall be known and may be cited as the hearsay rule.
HEIR - Generally, one who inherits property, real or personal.
HOLDER OF THE PRIVILEGE - (a) The client when he has no guardian or conservator; (b) A guardian or conservator of the client when the client has a guardian or conservator; (c) The personal representative of the client if the client is dead; (d) A successor, assign, trustee in dissolution, or any similar representative of a firm, association, organization, partnership, business trust, corporation, or public entity that is no longer in existence.
HUNG JURY - One so divided that they can't agree on a verdict.
HUSBAND-WIFE PRIVILEGE - An accused in a criminal proceeding has a privilege to prevent his spouse from testifying against him.
HYPOTHECATE - To pledge a thing without delivering it to the pledgee.
HYPOTHESIS - A supposition, assumption, or toehry.

I

I.E. (id est) - That is.
IB., OR IBID.(ibidem) - In the same place; used to refer to a legal reference previously cited to avoid repeating the entire citation.
ILLICIT - Prohibited; unlawful.
ILLUSORY - Deceiving by false appearance.
IMMUNITY - Exemption.
IMPEACH - To accuse, to dispute.
IMPEDIMENTS - Disabilities, or hindrances.
IMPLEAD - To sue or prosecute by due course of law.
IMPUTED - Attributed or charged to.
IN LOCO PARENTIS - In place of parent, a guardian.
IN TOTO - In the whole; completely.
INCHOATE - Imperfect; unfinished.
INCOMMUNICADO - Denial of the right of a prisoner to communicate with friends or relatives.
INCOMPETENT - One who is incapable of caring for his own affairs because he is mentally deficient or undeveloped.
INCRIMINATION - A matter will incriminate a person if it constitutes, or forms an essential part of, or, taken in connection with other matters disclosed, is a basis for a reasonable inference of such a violation of the laws of this State as to subject him to liability to punishment therefor, unless he has become for any reason permanently immune from punishment for such violation.
INCUMBRANCE - Generally a claim, lien, charge or liability attached to and binding real property.

INDEMNIFY - To secure against loss or damage; also, to make reimbursement to one for a loss already incurred by him.

INDEMNITY - An agreement to reimburse another person in case of an anticipated loss falling upon him.

INDICIA - Signs; indications.

INDICTMENT - An accusation in writing found and presented by a grand jury charging that a person has committed a crime.

INDORSE - To write a name on the back of a legal paper or document, generally, a negotiable instrument

INDUCEMENT - Cause or reason why a thing is done or that which incites the person to do the act or commit a crime; the motive for the criminal act.

INFANT - In civil cases one under 21 years of age.

INFORMATION - A formal accusation of crime made by a prosecuting attorney.

INFRA - Below, under; this word occurring by itself in a publication refers the reader to a future part of the publication.

INGRESS - The act of going into.

INJUNCTION - A writ or order by the court requiring a person, generally, to do or to refrain from doing an act.

INSOLVENT - The condition of a person who is unable to pay his debts.

INSTRUCTION - A direction given by the judge to the jury concerning the law of the case.

INTERIM - In the meantime; time intervening.

INTERLOCUTORY - Temporary, not final; something intervening between the commencement and the end of a suit which decides some point or matter, but is not a final decision of the whole controversy.

INTERROGATORIES - A series of formal written questions used in the examination of a party or a witness usually prior to a trial.

INTESTATE - A person who dies without a will.

INURE - To result, to take effect.

IPSO FACTO - By the fact iself; by the mere fact.

ISSUE (n.) The disputed point or question in a case,

J

JEOPARDY - Danger, hazard, peril.

JOINDER - Joining; uniting with another person in some legal steps or proceeding.

JOINT - United; combined.

JUDGE - Member or members or representative or representatives of a court conducting a trial or hearing at which evidence is introduced.

JUDGMENT - The official decision of a court of justice.

JUDICIAL OR JUDICIARY - Relating to or connected with the administration of justice.

JURAT - The clause written at the foot of an affidavit, stating when, where and before whom such affidavit was sworn.

JURISDICTION - The authority to hear and determine controversies between parties.

JURISPRUDENCE - The philosophy of law.

JURY - A body of persons legally selected to inquire into any matter of fact, and to render their verdict according to the evidence.

L

LACHES - The failure to diligently assert a right, which results in a refusal to allow relief.

LANDLORD AND TENANT - A phrase used to denote the legal relation existing between the owner and occupant of real estate.
LARCENY - Stealing personal property belonging to another.
LATENT - Hidden; that which does not appear on the face of a thing.
LAW - Includes constitutional, statutory, and decisional law.
LAWYER-CLIENT PRIVILEGE - (1) A "client" is a person, public officer, or corporation, association, or other organization or entity, either public or private, who is rendered professional legal services by a lawyer, or who consults a lawyer with a view to obtaining professional legal services from him; (2) A "lawyer" is a person authorized, or reasonably believed by the client to be authorized, to practice law in any state or nation; (3) A "representative of the lawyer" is one employed to assist the lawyer in the rendition of professional legal services; (4) A communication is "confidential" if not intended to be disclosed to third persons other than those to whom disclosure is in furtherance of the rendition of professional legal services to the client or those reasonably necessary for the transmission of the communication.

General rule of privilege - A client has a privilege to refuse to disclose and to prevent any other person from disclosing confidential communications made for the purpose of facilitating the rendition of professional legal services to the client, (1) between himself or his representative and his lawyer or his lawyer's representative, or (2) between his lawyer and the lawyer's representative, or (3) by him or his lawyer to a lawyer representing another in a matter of common interest, or (4) between representatives of the client or between the client and a representative of the client, or (5) between lawyers representing the client.
LEADING QUESTION - Question that suggests to the witness the answer that the examining party desires.
LEASE - A contract by which one conveys real estate for a limited time usually for a specified rent; personal property also may be leased.
LEGISLATION - The act of enacting laws.
LEGITIMATE - Lawful.
LESSEE - One to whom a lease is given.
LESSOR - One who grants a lease
LEVY - A collecting or exacting by authority.
LIABLE - Responsible; bound or obligated in law or equity.
LIBEL (v.) - To defame or injure a person's reputation by a published writing.
 (n.) - The initial pleading on the part of the plaintiff in an admiralty proceeding.
LIEN - A hold or claim which one person has upon the property of another as a security for some debt or charge.
LIQUIDATED - Fixed; settled.
LIS PENDENS - A pending civil or criminal action.
LITERAL - According to the language.
LITIGANT - A party to a lawsuit.
LITATION - A judicial controversy.
LOCUS - A place.
LOCUS DELICTI - Place of the crime.
LOCUS POENITENTIAE - The abandoning or giving up of one's intention to commit some crime before it is fully completed or abandoning a conspiracy before its purpose is accomplished.

M

MALFEASANCE - To do a wrongful act.
MALICE - The doing of a wrongful act Intentionally without just cause or excuse.

MANDAMUS - The name of a writ issued by a court to enforce the performance of some public duty.
MANDATORY (adj.) Containing a command.
MARITIME - Pertaining to the sea or to commerce thereon.
MARSHALING - Arranging or disposing of in order.
MAXIM - An established principle or proposition.
MINISTERIAL - That which involves obedience to instruction, but demands no special discretion, judgment or skill.
MISAPPROPRIATE - Dealing fraudulently with property entrusted to one.
MISDEMEANOR - A crime less than a felony and punishable by a fine or imprisonment for less than one year.
MISFEASANCE - Improper performance of a lawful act.
MISREPRESENTATION - An untrue representation of facts.
MITIGATE - To make or become less severe, harsh.
MITTIMUS - A warrant of commitment to prison.
MOOT (adj.) Unsettled, undecided, not necessary to be decided.
MORTGAGE - A conveyance of property upon condition, as security for the payment of a debt or the performance of a duty, and to become void upon payment or performance according to the stipulated terms.
MORTGAGEE - A person to whom property is mortgaged.
MORTGAGOR - One who gives a mortgage.
MOTION - In legal proceedings, a "motion" is an application, either written or oral, addressed to the court by a party to an action or a suit requesting the ruling of the court on a matter of law.
MUTUALITY - Reciprocation.

N

NEGLIGENCE - The failure to exercise that degree of care which an ordinarily prudent person would exercise under like circumstances.
NEGOTIABLE (instrument) - Any instrument obligating the payment of money which is transferable from one person to another by endorsement and delivery or by delivery only.
NEGOTIATE - To transact business; to transfer a negotiable instrument; to seek agreement for the amicable disposition of a controversy or case.
NOLLE PROSEQUI - A formal entry upon the record, by the plaintiff in a civil suit or the prosecuting officer in a criminal action, by which he declares that he "will no further prosecute" the case.
NOLO CONTENDERE - The name of a plea in a criminal action, having the same effect as a plea of guilty; but not constituting a direct admission of guilt.
NOMINAL - Not real or substantial.
NOMINAL DAMAGES - Award of a trifling sum where no substantial injury is proved to have been sustained.
NONFEASANCE - Neglect of duty.
NOVATION - The substitution of a new debt or obligation for an existing one.
NUNC PRO TUNC - A phrase applied to acts allowed to be done after the time when they should be done, with a retroactive effect.("Now for then.")

O

OATH - Oath includes affirmation or declaration under penalty of perjury.
OBITER DICTUM - Opinion expressed by a court on a matter not essentially involved in a case and hence not a decision; also called dicta, if plural.

OBJECT (v.) - To oppose as improper or illegal and referring the question of its propriety or legality to the court.
OBLIGATION - A legal duty, by which a person is bound to do or not to do a certain thing.
OBLIGEE - The person to whom an obligation is owed.
OBLIGOR - The person who is to perform the obligation.
OFFER (v.) - To present for acceptance or rejection.
 (n.) - A proposal to do a thing, usually a proposal to make a contract.
OFFICIAL INFORMATION - Information within the custody or control of a department or agency of the government the disclosure of which is shown to be contrary to the public interest.
OFFSET - A deduction.
ONUS PROBANDI - Burden of proof.
OPINION - The statement by a judge of the decision reached in a case, giving the law as applied to the case and giving reasons for the judgment; also a belief or view.
OPTION - The exercise of the power of choice; also a privilege existing in one person, for which he has paid money, which gives him the right to buy or sell real or personal property at a given price within a specified time.
ORDER - A rule or regulation; every direction of a court or judge made or entered in writing but not including a judgment.
ORDINANCE - Generally, a rule established by authority; also commonly used to designate the legislative acts of a municipal corporation.
ORIGINAL - Writing or recording itself or any counterpart intended to have the same effect by a person executing or issuing it. An "original" of a photograph includes the negative or any print therefrom. If data are stored in a computer or similar device, any printout or other output readable by sight, shown to reflect the data accurately, is an "original."
OVERT - Open, manifest.

P

PANEL - A group of jurors selected to serve during a term of the court.
PARENS PATRIAE - Sovereign power of a state to protect or be a guardian over children and incompetents.
PAROL - Oral or verbal.
PAROLE - To release one in prison before the expiration of his sentence, conditionally.
PARITY - Equality in purchasing power between the farmer and other segments of the economy.
PARTITION - A legal division of real or personal property between one or more owners.
PARTNERSHIP - An association of two or more persons to carry on as co-owners a business for profit.
PATENT (adj.) - Evident.
 (n.) - A grant of some privilege, property, or authority, made by the government or sovereign of a country to one or more individuals.
PECULATION - Stealing.
PECUNIARY - Monetary.
PENULTIMATE - Next to the last.
PER CURIAM - A phrase used in the report of a decision to distinguish an opinion of the whole court from an opinion written by any one judge.
PER SE - In itself; taken alone.
PERCEIVE - To acquire knowledge through one's senses.
PEREMPTORY - Imperative; absolute.
PERJURY - To lie or state falsely under oath.

PERPETUITY - Perpetual existence; also the quality or condition of an estate limited so that it will not take effect or vest within the period fixed by law.
PERSON - Includes a natural person, firm, association, organization, partnership, business trust, corporation, or public entity.
PERSONAL PROPERTY - Includes money, goods, chattels, things in action, and evidences of debt.
PERSONALTY - Short term for personal property.
PETITION - An application in writing for an order of the court, stating the circumstances upon which it is founded and requesting any order or other relief from a court.
PLAINTIFF - A person who brings a court action.
PLEA - A pleading in a suit or action.
PLEADINGS - Formal allegations made by the parties of their respective claims and defenses, for the judgment of the court.
PLEDGE - A deposit of personal property as a security for the performance of an act.
PLEDGEE - The party to whom goods are delivered in pledge.
PLEDGOR - The party delivering goods in pledge.
PLENARY - Full; complete.
POLICE POWER - Inherent power of the state or its political subdivisions to enact laws within constitutional limits to promote the general welfare of society or the community.
POLLING THE JURY - Call the names of persons on a jury and requiring each juror to declare what his verdict is before it is legally recorded.
POST MORTEM - After death.
POWER OF ATTORNEY - A writing authorizing one to act for another.
PRECEPT - An order, warrant, or writ issued to an officer or body of officers, commanding him or them to do some act within the scope of his or their powers.
PRELIMINARY FACT - Fact upon the existence or nonexistence of which depends the admissibility or inadmissibility of evidence. The phrase "the admissibility or inadmissibility of evidence" includes the qualification or disqualification of a person to be a witness and the existence or non-existence of a privilege.
PREPONDERANCE - Outweighing.
PRESENTMENT - A report by a grand jury on something they have investigated on their own knowledge.
PRESUMPTION - An assumption of fact resulting from a rule of law which requires such fact to be assumed from another fact or group of facts found or otherwise established in the action.
PRIMA FACUE - At first sight.
PRIMA FACIE CASE - A case where the evidence is very patent against the defendant.
PRINCIPAL - The source of authority or rights; a person primarily liable as differentiated from "principle" as a primary or basic doctrine.
PRO AND CON - For and against.
PRO RATA - Proportionally.
PROBATE - Relating to proof, especially to the proof of wills.
PROBATIVE - Tending to prove.
PROCEDURE - In law, this term generally denotes rules which are established by the Federal, State, or local Governments regarding the types of pleading and courtroom practice which must be followed by the parties involved in a criminal or civil case.
PROCLAMATION - A public notice by an official of some order, intended action, or state of facts.

PROFFERED EVIDENCE - The admissibility or inadmissibility of which is dependent upon the existence or nonexistence of a preliminary fact.
PROMISSORY (NOTE) - A promise in writing to pay a specified sum at an expressed time, or on demand, or at sight, to a named person, or to his order, or bearer.
PROOF - The establishment by evidence of a requisite degree of belief concerning a fact in the mind of the trier of fact or the court.
PROPERTY - Includes both real and personal property.
PROPRIETARY (adj.) - Relating or pertaining to ownership; usually a single owner.
PROSECUTE - To carry on an action or other judicial proceeding; to proceed against a person criminally.
PROVISO - A limitation or condition in a legal instrument.
PROXIMATE - Immediate; nearest
PUBLIC EMPLOYEE - An officer, agent, or employee of a public entity.
PUBLIC ENTITY - Includes a national, state, county, city and county, city, district, public authority, public agency, or any other political subdivision or public corporation, whether foreign or domestic.
PUBLIC OFFICIAL - Includes an official of a political dubdivision of such state or territory and of a municipality.
PUNITIVE - Relating to punishment.

Q

QUASH - To make void.
QUASI - As if; as it were.
QUID PRO QUO - Something for something; the giving of one valuable thing for another.
QUITCLAIM (v.) - To release or relinquish claim or title to, especially in deeds to realty.
QUO WARRANTO - A legal procedure to test an official's right to a public office or the right to hold a franchise, or to hold an office in a domestic corporation.

R

RATIFY - To approve and sanction.
REAL PROPERTY - Includes lands, tenements, and hereditaments.
REALTY - A brief term for real property.
REBUT - To contradict; to refute, especially by evidence and arguments.
RECEIVER - A person who is appointed by the court to receive, and hold in trust property in litigation.
RECIDIVIST - Habitual criminal.
RECIPROCAL - Mutual.
RECOUPMENT - To keep back or get something which is due; also, it is the right of a defendant to have a deduction from the amount of the plaintiff's damages because the plaintiff has not fulfilled his part of the same contract.
RECROSS EXAMINATION - Examination of a witness by a cross-examiner subsequent to a redirect examination of the witness.
REDEEM - To release an estate or article from mortgage or pledge by paying the debt for which it stood as security.
REDIRECT EXAMINATION - Examination of a witness by the direct examiner subsequent to the cross-examination of the witness.
REFEREE - A person to whom a cause pending in a court is referred by the court, to take testimony, hear the parties, and report thereon to the court.

REFERENDUM - A method of submitting an important legislative or administrative matter to a direct vote of the people.
RELEVANT EVIDENCE - Evidence including evidence relevant to the credulity of a witness or hearsay declarant, having any tendency in reason to prove or disprove any disputed fact that is of consequence to the determination of the action.
REMAND - To send a case back to the lower court from which it came, for further proceedings.
REPLEVIN - An action to recover goods or chattels wrongfully taken or detained.
REPLY (REPLICATION) - Generally, a reply is what the plaintiff or other person who has instituted proceedings says in answer to the defendant's case.
RE JUDICATA - A thing judicially acted upon or decided.
RES ADJUDICATA - Doctrine that an issue or dispute litigated and determined in a case between the opposing parties is deemed permanently decided between these parties.
RESCIND (RECISSION) - To avoid or cancel a contract.
RESPONDENT - A defendant in a proceeding in chancery or admiralty; also, the person who contends against the appeal in a case.
RESTITUTION - In equity, it is the restoration of both parties to their original condition (when practicable), upon the rescission of a contract for fraud or similar cause.
RETROACTIVE (RETROSPECTIVE) - Looking back; effective as of a prior time.
REVERSED - A term used by appellate courts to indicate that the decision of the lower court in the case before it has been set aside.
REVOKE - To recall or cancel.
RIPARIAN (RIGHTS) - The rights of a person owning land containing or bordering on a water course or other body of water, such as lakes and rivers.

S

SALE - A contract whereby the ownership of property is transferred from one person to another for a sum of money or for any consideration.
SANCTION - A penalty or punishment provided as a means of enforcing obedience to a law; also, an authorization.
SATISFACTION - The discharge of an obligation by paying a party what is due to him; or what is awarded to him by the judgment of a court or otherwise.
SCIENTER - Knowingly; also, it is used in pleading to denote the defendant's guilty knowledge.
SCINTILLA - A spark; also the least particle.
SECRET OF STATE - Governmental secret relating to the national defense or the international relations of the United States.
SECURITY - Indemnification; the term is applied to an obligation, such as a mortgage or deed of trust, given by a debtor to insure the payment or performance of his debt, by furnishing the creditor with a resource to be used in case of the debtor's failure to fulfill the principal obligation.
SENTENCE - The judgment formally pronounced by the court or judge upon the defendant after his conviction in a criminal prosecution.
SET-OFF - A claim or demand which one party in an action credits against the claim of the opposing party.
SHALL and MAY - "Shall" is mandatory and "may" is permissive.
SITUS - Location.
SOVEREIGN - A person, body or state in which independent and supreme authority is vested.
STARE DECISIS - To follow decided cases.

STATE - "State" means this State, unless applied to the different parts of the United States. In the latter case, it includes any state, district, commonwealth, territory or insular possession of the United States, including the District of Columbia.

STATEMENT - (a) Oral or written verbal expression or (b) nonverbal conduct of a person intended by him as a substitute for oral or written verbal expression.

STATUTE - An act of the legislature. Includes a treaty.

STATUTE OF LIMITATION - A statute limiting the time to bring an action after the right of action has arisen.

STAY - To hold in abeyance an order of a court.

STIPULATION - Any agreement made by opposing attorneys regulating any matter incidental to the proceedings or trial.

SUBORDINATION (AGREEMENT) - An agreement making one's rights inferior to or of a lower rank than another's.

SUBORNATION - The crime of procuring a person to lie or to make false statements to a court.

SUBPOENA - A writ or order directed to a person, and requiring his attendance at a particular time and place to testify as a witness.

SUBPOENA DUCES TECUM - A subpoena used, not only for the purpose of compelling witnesses to attend in court, but also requiring them to bring with them books or documents which may be in their possession, and which may tend to elucidate the subject matter of the trial.

SUBROGATION - The substituting of one for another as a creditor, the new creditor succeeding to the former's rights.

SUBSIDY - A government grant to assist a private enterprise deemed advantageous to the public.

SUI GENERIS - Of the same kind.

SUIT - Any civil proceeding by a person or persons against another or others in a court of justice by which the plaintiff pursues the remedies afforded him by law.

SUMMONS - A notice to a defendant that an action against him has been commenced and requiring him to appear in court and answer the complaint.

SUPRA - Above; this word occurring by itself in a book refers the reader to a previous part of the book.

SURETY - A person who binds himself for the payment of a sum of money, or for the performance of something else, for another.

SURPLUSAGE - Extraneous or unnecessary matter.

SURVIVORSHIP - A term used when a person becomes entitled to property by reason of his having survived another person who had an interest in the property.

SUSPEND SENTENCE - Hold back a sentence pending good behavior of prisoner.

SYLLABUS - A note prefixed to a report, especially a case, giving a brief statement of the court's ruling on different issues of the case.

T

TALESMAN - Person summoned to fill a panel of jurors.

TENANT - One who holds or possesses lands by any kind of right or title; also, one who has the temporary use and occupation of real property owned by another person (landlord), the duration and terms of his tenancy being usually fixed by an instrument called "a lease."

TENDER - An offer of money; an expression of willingness to perform a contract according to its terms.

TERM - When used with reference to a court, it signifies the period of time during which the court holds a session, usually of several weeks or months duration.

TESTAMENTARY - Pertaining to a will or the administration of a will.
TESTATOR (male)
TESTATRIX (female) - One who makes or has made a testament or will.
TESTIFY (TESTIMONY) - To give evidence under oath as a witness.
TO WIT - That is to say; namely.
TORT - Wrong; injury to the person.
TRANSITORY - Passing from place to place.
TRESPASS - Entry into another's ground, illegally.
TRIAL - The examination of a cause, civil or criminal, before a judge who has jurisdiction over it, according to the laws of the land.
TRIER OF FACT - Includes (a) the jury and (b) the court when the court is trying an issue of fact other than one relating to the admissibility of evidence.
TRUST - A right of property, real or personal, held by one party for the benefit of another.
TRUSTEE - One who lawfully holds property in custody for the benefit of another.

U

UNAVAILABLE AS A WITNESS - The declarant is (1) Exempted or precluded on the ground of privilege from testifying concerning the matter to which his statement is relevant; (2) Disqualified from testifying to the matter; (3) Dead or unable to attend or to testify at the hearing because of then existing physical or mental illness or infirmity; (4) Absent from the hearing and the court is unable to compel his attendance by its process; or (5) Absent from the hearing and the proponent of his statement has exercised reasonable diligence but has been unable to procure his attendance by the court's process.
ULTRA VIRES - Acts beyond the scope and power of a corporation, association, etc.
UNILATERAL - One-sided; obligation upon, or act of one party.
USURY - Unlawful interest on a loan.

V

VACATE - To set aside; to move out.
VARIANCE - A discrepancy or disagreement between two instruments or two aspects of the same case, which by law should be consistent.
VENDEE - A purchaser or buyer.
VENDOR - The person who transfers property by sale, particularly real estate; the term "seller" is used more commonly for one who sells personal property.
VENIREMEN - Persons ordered to appear to serve on a jury or composing a panel of jurors.
VENUE - The place at which an action is tried, generally based on locality or judicial district in which an injury occurred or a material fact happened.
VERDICT - The formal decision or finding of a jury.
VERIFY - To confirm or substantiate by oath.
VEST - To accrue to.
VOID - Having no legal force or binding effect.
VOIR DIRE - Preliminary examination of a witness or a juror to test competence, interest, prejudice, etc.

W

WAIVE - To give up a right.
WAIVER - The intentional or voluntary relinquishment of a known right.
WARRANT (WARRANTY) (v.) - To promise that a certain fact or state of facts, in relation to the subject matter, is, or shall be, as it is represented to be.

WARRANT (n.) - A writ issued by a judge, or other competent authority, addressed to a sheriff, or other officer, requiring him to arrest the person therein named, and bring him before the judge or court to answer or be examined regarding the offense with which he is charged.

WRIT - An order or process issued in the name of the sovereign or in the name of a court or judicial officer, commanding the performance or nonperformance of some act.

WRITING - Handwriting, typewriting, printing, photostating, photographing and every other means of recording upon any tangible thing any form of communication or representation, including letters, words, pictures, sounds, or symbols, or combinations thereof.

WRITINGS AND RECORDINGS - Consists of letters, words, or numbers, or their equivalent, set down by handwriting, typewriting, printing, photostating, photographing, magnetic impulse, mechanical or electronic recording, or other form of data compilation.

Y

YEA AND NAY - Yes and no.

YELLOW DOG CONTRACT - A contract by which employer requires employee to sign an instrument promising as condition that he will not join a union during its continuance, and will be discharged if he does join.

Z

ZONING - The division of a city by legislative regulation into districts and the prescription and application in each district of regulations having to do with structural and architectural designs of buildings and of regulations prescribing use to which buildings within designated districts may be put.

www.ingramcontent.com/pod-product-compliance
Lightning Source LLC
Chambersburg PA
CBHW082209300426

44117CB00016B/2726